TIJUANA
TO THE
CROSS

SANDEE MOGLE

Copyright © 2021 Sandee Mogle
ISBN: 978-0-578-96116-3

Cover Artwork by Kaitlin White Griffis and Shane Minor

First Edition

DEDICATION

For more than thirty years, I have expressed the desire to write my story to my immediate family and friends. Most family members truly do not want to read intimate details about their mom, sister, or aunt. My sons have encouraged me to write my story – the evolution of the business traveler along with my own evolution from Tijuana to flying first class to Paris as a Child of The King. Many details were a hard pill to swallow. To Mark and Rachael, Matt and Bethany (it's alphabetical guys – not playing favorites!), thank you for believing in me and for your approval at the sharing of such a personal journey.

Trish Burdick, you have been my faithful content editor! You have read this in its entirety at least twelve times, asking me questions about what I truly meant and was trying to convey. You were like my counselor, probing to get to my soul. I know in your heart, like mine, you feel that lives can be changed from this story.

Rachael Mogle, my line editor, what a treasure you are. Trish and I had the words down but you brought them to clarity and life! It is not an accident that as you edited the final chapters you were carrying my first grandchild, who will be called Phillip Mogle. Tears upon tears of joy have been poured into this book!

Rick Orcutt and Shane Minor, thank you for your unwavering desire to bring my dream to life. Your creativity, ingenuity, research, and insight made Tijuana to the Cross a published reality!

To God be the Glory

TABLE OF CONTENTS

PART ONE

ELEVEN MILES FROM TIJUANA

The traffic on a Tuesday night moved at a normal pace as we pulled up to the San Ysidro-Tijuana International Border crossing. San Ysidro was the busiest of the international U.S. border crossings in the 1950s and '60s. The agent leaned in and asked my dad what the purpose of our visit to Tijuana was.

"Just dinner," he answered.

The guard asked each of us where we were born, then, out of boredom, waved us on. It was the early '60's. Drugs were on the radar, but terrorism was not even a blip.

We weaved our way through the crazy traffic to a restaurant I called Tony's, better known as Polermo's. It was directly across from the beautiful Jai Alai Palace. Dad dropped Mom and me off at the front door and pulled around back. We were always greeted by waiters wearing white serving jackets and gloves.

"Welcome lady and little one."

We were well-known to the staff of this famous restaurant. The maître d' guided us to a white linen-draped table. Mom ordered a gin martini for herself and a Shirley Temple for me, complete with the coveted cherry on a fancy toothpick. Dad appeared a bit later, gin martini in hand.

The brass and glass salad cart appeared at our table where the performance of making the restaurant's famous Caesar salad began. Raw egg, anchovies, garlic, olive oil, and lemon juice were all magically whisked together, drizzled over fresh crisp romaine, and served elegantly on an ice-cold platter with shavings of aged parmesan cheese. Chilled forks cradled in a perfectly folded white linen napkin were offered to each one of us. I'm sure the adult entrées of thick sizzling filets and seasonal lobster served with the coveted melted butter and delicate abalone were magnificent, but nothing could match my fabulous plain spaghetti served with a yummy butter and garlic sauce. To me, going across the Tijuana border every month was an absolute delight. It never dawned on me why we went.

During the late '50s and early '60s, Tijuana was what I would consider safe, but only if you stayed on the main streets like Revolución Boulevard. *Jai Alai* (pronounced "Hi Li" and dubbed "the fastest sport in the world") was an alternative to horse and dog racing, also with betting. Picture an indoor stadium similar to a racquetball court with the crowd in stadium seating behind a glass wall or chain link fence. The two players slung the ball using a hand-held wicker device that looked like a long scoop. This was a very fast-paced game, the ball often traveling more than 100 mph. The record is 188 mph. Watching this sport was popular among the Hollywood crowd, so seeing Sammy Davis Jr., Dean Martin, Bob Hope, Judy Garland, Frank Sinatra, and other beautiful people from the Jai Alai Palace when crossing the street to dine at Palermo's was not uncommon.

We lived in San Diego, south of the Naval base in National City. Our home was a typical post-WWII house that proliferated throughout Southern California. The need for quick housing was great. Most homes had a living room, a kitchen, two bedrooms, one bathroom, aluminum windows, stucco siding, and a single-car unattached garage. Insulation and air conditioning were unheard of and certainly not needed in the temperate climate of San Diego. These are the homes you now see on HGTV being remodeled and sold for $900,000. Location, location, location. Back then, I never thought that living less than fifteen minutes from the Pacific Ocean was a luxury. It was just…there.

My family's business was running a liquor store. Right before I was to enter third grade, Dad told us he had sold the liquor store and that we were moving. They had owned the store for years, but downtown San Diego was becoming seedy with hobos, drunks, sleezy bars, and tattoo parlors. As a child, all I remember is one day we left everything behind at our old home except for our clothing and stuffed animals. We drove to our brand-new home in Chula Vista, eleven miles from the Tijuana border.

I walked into a home where everything was new – I mean *everything*. Pots, pans, refrigerator, stove, furniture, drapes, lamps, sheets, towels, mattresses, bedspreads, pillows. And I had my own bedroom with two windows, which proved to be great for sneaking out when I hit my teenage years. We started making our monthly trips to Tijuana right after this move.

Along with the new house, Mom and Dad bought a new liquor store, which was quite beautiful. It was so clean and uncluttered. A refrigerated glass display case ran the entire width of the back of the store. The glass glistened, bright and shiny. We had our own square bottles with private labels for scotch, bourbon, gin, and vodka, all named for the liquor store – The Square Bottle. The back room became the neighborhood gathering place, kind of like Mayberry RFD but with liquor.

After moving to Chula Vista, this liquor store would prove to make me popular in high school, for all the wrong reasons. As I got older and looked back at this move, I did wonder where they got all the money to make such a huge and complete transition. New home. New liquor store. New everything.

I never got my answer.

It wasn't until much later that I realized why we went to Tijuana every month – we were running a trunk full of liquor down to Tony's. Tijuana had plenty of liquor on its own, so perhaps it was the quality or selection of liquor that Tony's clientele came to expect. I've often wondered what would've happened if the border guard had asked us to open our trunk. Did my dad think the risk was worth it with his family in the car? Maybe Dad thought a little bonus slipped into the guard's hand would give us the go-ahead. Fortunately, we were never stopped.

After years of our monthly Tijuana travels, the trips stopped. I never heard why. Perhaps Tony sold Palermo's and the new owner wasn't in need of my dad's special stock.

Squinting into the setting sun from our Chula Vista living room window, we could see a teeny-tiny sliver of San Diego Bay, the Pacific Ocean, and, off to the southwest, the twinkling night lights of Tijuana. The city lights covering the Mexican hillside were beautiful. As a child, I didn't know that under those lights were emaciated orphans and old women living in a type of poverty I could not imagine, where cardboard boxes become homes and meals are formed from digging through garbage dumps for the slightest bit of anything edible. I wouldn't discover this horror until I visited the dump years later.

Our new neighborhood felt upscale to me, but it was quite basic. Most homes were 1,200 square feet with three bedrooms and one-and-a-half bathrooms. Our kitchen was small, but it had a great window over the sink to view the sunset. Like our old home, the exterior was stucco with aluminum sliding windows, and we had a double-car attached garage. The standard lot size was fifty feet by one-hundred feet. Each home could be no closer than five feet from the side of the property line, so we all had ten feet between our houses.

With minimal rain each year, we truly had few home repairs. There was no ice, mold, mildew, tornadoes, hurricanes, or major temperature changes. People were concerned about earthquakes, and though there have been some horrific ones, we never knew when they were coming, so they weren't a concern or fear. I don't recall Dad ever changing out gutters as they rarely served their purpose. The only thing I remember that required maintenance were the aluminum window tracks. The moist, salty sea air eventually pitted them with small white bumps. We sanded them down so that the windows wouldn't get hung up. As an adult now having lived in North Carolina, New Jersey, Virginia, Alabama, and Colorado, I realize that home maintenance in Southern California was a piece of cake!

Life was laid back in Southern California, as it was in most parts of the country. In the early summer hours, we ran outside to play and came home for a grilled cheese or bologna sandwich on fresh white, fluffy Wonder Bread that stuck to the roof of our mouths. This gourmet fluff sold for twenty cents a loaf in 1959. Its wrapper, printed with red, yellow, and blue balloons, was a staple in all my friends' kitchens. After lunch, we headed back outside, not returning until dinnertime.

Days consisted of building forts, running all over the neighborhood playing cowboys and Indians, and selling lemonade for five cents in the front yard. After dinner, we'd be back outside playing hide-and-go-seek until it was time for bed. We didn't have the joy of catching lightning bugs in Southern California, but that was a fair trade-off for few bug bites and no humidity.

Everyone slept with their windows and doors open. Perhaps we latched the screen door shut when someone remembered to do so. Parents wanting to know where we were or who we were playing with was of no concern; our neighborhood and community were safe places. The moms I knew made inexpensive meals like kidney bean stew, meatloaf with lots of breadcrumbs mushed in, and – my favorite – hamburger gravy over mashed potatoes. These meals were followed by a baked one-layer cake that went a long way to feed four to five kids. It was a frugal neighborhood with many modest habits set from post-WWII upbringings.

The phrase stay-at-home mom was not yet part of anyone's vocabulary, but it was the norm – except for my mom. She and Dad had a unique arrangement.

At 10:00 a.m., Dad opened the liquor store, which was eight minutes from our home. He worked until 2:00 p.m., when Mom came and took over. Dad went about town, visiting and talking to store owners and the folks in the bank. He'd stop by the local drug store and chat with the pharmacist and everyone else. Next, he would go to the grocery store owned by a local family, then he would head home. At 6:00 p.m., a hired man named Dennis would come and relieve Mom and close at 10:00 p.m. Dennis, a mail carrier by day, worked for them at night faithfully for over fifteen years. My parents had a great life!

Dad was the cook in our family, and he was superb. He greeted Mom with a gin martini when she walked through the kitchen door at 6:15, and they usually had another one before dinner. I got used to eating dinner with them around 7:30, but my first dinner was at 6:00.

The delicious, wonderful meals I mentioned above – kidney bean stew, meatloaf, and hamburger gravy – came from across the street. This saint of a mom fed me, along with her five children, for years. It all started around fifth grade when I realized they ate at precisely 6:00 p.m. every night.

We would often all be outside playing when they would be called in for dinner. I had to go home to no food and a noisy stomach. Like a dog slowly sneaking his way into a room he knows he shouldn't be in, I would go knock on the family's kitchen door at 6:30 to see if they could play again. Of course, they would just be finishing dessert. I was always invited in for a piece of cake. Little by little, I reduced my time frame, knocking on the door at 6:20, 6:15, and so on. Every time I knocked, the older boys would tease me.

"I bet that's Sandee. Somebody better move over!"

When their oldest son enlisted in the Navy, I eventually had my own chair at the table for the entire dinner. Heaven! This family became my normal place. After dinner, we girls would do the dishes and watch the mom and her husband leave for a walk around the block every night. I thought it was so romantic. Afterward, I'd go home and pretend to be hungry at 7:30 as Dad served Mom and I dinner, complete with another gin martini for them.

I guess they thought I just had a small appetite.

DAD

Dad was raised in Cincinnati, Ohio, by strong German parents. I know so little of my dad's side of the family. I only visited them twice, once when I was three years old and again at age eleven. I don't even know how many brothers or sisters he had. I do know my grandmother was called G'ma Rose.

I guess you could call Dad the black sheep of the family. Born in 1907, he was the only one to ever leave Ohio. From the tales I remember, he rode the rails to Chicago in his early twenties. Prohibition was in full swing, and Dad learned to buy liquor under the table or in a speakeasy. Perhaps the excitement, danger, and intrigue of Chicago during this time was what sparked his interest in the liquor business. Afterward, something drew him to Southern California – who or what, I have no idea. He must have made money somewhere, enough to buy a liquor store in downtown San Diego, not far from the Navy ships and next to a corner bar called the Circus Circus.

San Diego was a Navy town, bursting with activity in the middle of WWII. Even though my dad owned the liquor store, money was tight. He spent his nights sleeping on a cot in the back room. Everyone was called to work for the war effort. Liquor store hours were limited, so he also worked part-time at Ryan Aeronautical, where he met my mom. They later married in April of 1947.

My dad was a man's man. He smoked Camel cigarettes, drank whiskey, and rarely – if ever – shared his emotions with my mom, my brother, or me. I knew he loved me, although how I knew, I'm not sure. He was always proud of me, that's for certain.

Dad was hard on my brother, Ronnie. I constantly got Ronnie into trouble. I'd do something I wasn't supposed to do and then blame it on him. Mom and Dad never questioned me nor thought I possibly could be lying. One time when I was six years old, Ronnie and I were in our grandfather's workshop. I picked up a big knife, like a machete.

"Sandee, put that down and quit waving it at me or I'll tell," Ronnie said.

"Go ahead, I don't care. You know I won't get in trouble. You will," I replied.

I started laughing, poking the knife at him in midair. My dad must have heard us and came around the corner.

"What's going on?" my dad asked.

"She's got a knife and she was going to stab me with it," Ronnie answered.

Dad looked at me. I clenched the knife in my right hand behind my back.

"Sandee, do you have a knife?"

I looked at my dad straight in the face.

"No, Ronnie is lying!"

My dad turned to my brother.

"Ronnie, go to your room."

My dad never asked what was behind my back. Resentment started to grow between my brother and me.

In eighth and ninth grade, Ronnie was sent to Brown Military Academy, a boarding school in Pacific Beach. I remember going to visit and watching the students march in an orderly line across the parade field.

Years later, I learned Ronnie was actually my half-brother. Our mom had been widowed with a child. Perhaps this was why my dad was so hard on Ronnie. When Ronnie moved back home for a short time, they had their final argument.

Ronnie was seven years older than I was. He and his gorgeous guy friends were all into the coolest of cars – hot rods, model T's, '56 Chevys. I loved it when they all hung out at our house, although they always ignored me, the squirt kid sister. One afternoon, my brother and his buddies were washing their cars in our driveway.

Ronnie turned the hose nozzle to the off position, but he left the water on. The built-up pressure ripped a small hole in the hose. This was the final blow-up between him and Dad. When it comes to a father's relationship with their son, it couldn't have been more insignificant. But that was it.

My brother moved out and lived with our grandmother for his last year of high school. Having the house to myself, I truly became the spoiled brat. Years later, my cousins and aunt informed me of all I had done to Ronnie, things that my mom and I had totally blocked out. I realized how horrible I had been to my brother and sent an apology letter to him, asking for forgiveness. Fortunately, he accepted.

As an adult, I now can see how my dad's aloofness toward me, his absence of expectations and boundaries, and his lack of a moral code of right or wrong allowed me to run wild. More than anything else, I wanted him to be the strong cowboy, the kind I saw on TV that rescues the girl. I wanted him to be my prince, my knight in shining armor until the right man for me came along. I now know that dads have an incredible role in the purity and self-respect a daughter has and holds for herself.

I remember only one time where my dad offered what might be construed as parental advice. I was twelve years old and flying for the first time all by myself. I was going from San Diego to Chicago to visit my aunt, uncle, and two cousins.

"If a man sits next to you and puts his hand on your knee, move."

This was his one piece of advice and the only information I ever received regarding the sex talk from Mom or Dad.

Years later, my niece recalled a time when she crawled up onto my father's lap. He was puffing away on his cigarette, and she was fanning away the smoke and gagging.

"This bothering you, kid?" he said.

She nodded, and he stubbed it out in his ashtray.

A few minutes later, he lit up a new cigarette and continued to puff away. He loved her, but it was a different place and time.

I never questioned my dad's love for me, but I do wonder about the depth of his love since there was never any guidance or correction. He and my mom just wanted me to be happy. That gave me an excuse never to face anything, commit to anything, or fight for something worth fighting for, like a marriage. For the first thirty-one years of my life, my way of handling any conflict was to leave.

If I didn't like something, I left.

Problem solved.

For some reason, my mom always yielded to my dad's behavior, letting him take the lead. She was submissive. I think she knew what was coming from him, usually verbal rants. When we went out to restaurants, the routine was always the same.

If the food took too long, Dad would get irate and complain. He'd march into the kitchen and yell at the staff. Then, he'd buy the chef a drink, and they would end up being buddies – every time. Mom and I were left to fend for ourselves. Eventually, he would come back, telling us what great guys were back in the kitchen. We'd eat, they would drink more, and then we'd be ready to leave. Fortunately, he always let Mom drive. In the car, he'd often get angry about something else and demand she pull over so he could get out to walk home.

I began to think my mom was a saint.

MOM

Mom was born in 1910 in Oregon. Her grandparents helped settle the state, heading across the country with tens of thousands of pioneers on the Oregon Trail in the 1850s.

My mom's dad was an attorney and her mom graduated from the University of Oregon with a bachelor's degree in music. Years later, for health reasons, they moved my mom and her brother to Phoenix, Arizona. After graduating from high school, my mom attended the local trade school and my uncle clocked in flight hours for his future career as a pilot. A great job opportunity took Mom and her parents to San Diego, where she met her first husband. They had a baby boy, my brother Ronnie. Four years later, Mom's husband died from pneumonia.

A beautiful, now single woman with a baby at the height of WWII could have led to an immensely dire and difficult situation. Fortunately, Mom's parents opened their home, providing the warmth, support, and love Mom and Ronnie needed. Mom landed a job at Ryan Aeronautical, where she met my dad. After dating for a year, they married. I came along shortly after.

My childhood memories of Mom are filled with laughter and her beautiful smile. She also had a wicked sense of humor. She wrote amusing complaint letters to companies, one being to a bra company that guaranteed to hold your shape nicely, even during strenuous exercise like playing tennis. Mom's letter informed them that the bra did not live up to her expectations. She explained that while gardening, out popped one of her breasts, and then, to her dismay, out popped the other. The company promptly responded that her letter left them rolling on the floor and they would be happy to send her several styles to try to meet her expectations. In the family liquor store, Mom was in charge of the greeting cards and cocktail napkins, all extremely hilarious and a bit risqué.

I don't know if Dad saw Mom as competition or just a woman who was bold, intelligent, and outgoing, but he never showed her any physical attention. Slowly, her light dimmed. I remember times when she tried to cuddle up with him or just put her arm through his.

"Cut it out," he would say.

I'll never forget the hurt look on her face.

They did love having people over to our home. Dad always cooked the meal. Opening our home to friends was something they truly enjoyed together.

Years later, they sold the liquor store and moved back to Arizona. Once Dad passed away in 1979, it was like Mom was a free bird, getting involved in communities as she moved around Arizona. She became the manager of the Kearny Chamber of Commerce and the Pinal County Development Board. She also worked at the Phoenix Zoo and the Trading Post in Sedona, where she started the Western Welcome Service. Mom was an adventurer at heart, and I now see so much of her in myself.

GENERIC PRAYERS

My parents delighted in having people over for dinner, usually on Saturday nights. After they ate, they all played poker. I loved their poker chip holder, a round carousel holding thirty chips with two columns each of red, blue, and white. For some reason, this silly thing still brings me comfort today, remembering the laughter and people in our home. I don't use it and it's now covered in dust, but it makes me think of Mom and Dad.

Dad loved to cook the vast majority of the time, but Mom always wore the chef's hat for Thanksgiving, Christmas, and Easter. We'd set up a long, eight-foot table in the living room where Mom displayed her nice silver, plates, and linens. Those holidays still evoke memories of beautiful days, all the windows open with a light breeze, welcoming people over who didn't have a place to celebrate their holiday, like the local pharmacist going through a divorce or the couple whose children lived far away. As aloof as my dad was to my mom, he had a kind heart to folks who would otherwise be alone.

He sat at the end of the table, carved the turkey or sliced the ham, then said his prayer. It was always generic, as if it were an obligatory thing to do before taking a bite.

"Thank you, Lord, for this food we are about to receive. Amen."

Is this it? Is this all there is? I wondered.

I always had this gnawing feeling of wanting to know more. What was the purpose of Easter and Christmas? I had Thanksgiving down pat, as we learned about the Pilgrims and Indians in school. Sure, we also sang about the baby Jesus and the Nativity scene that was commonly viewed in people's yards. It was tradition, but it meant nothing to me. Easter and Christmas left me with a hollow feeling. What was it?

When I was in high school, I received a new tennis racquet one Christmas. After the generic prayer was said, the food was eaten, and the dishes were cleared, I excused myself to go to the school and hit balls against the backstop with my new racquet. While walking there, I had a nagging question in my gut.

Is this all there is?

Maybe.

But even growing up in a godless void, I still had questions in my heart.

Does God plant something deep inside of us to long for, to yearn for Him? Is it a parent's responsibility to talk to their children about God, heaven, life, and death?

As a parent today, I know it is. But back then, it seemed as though the child was left to figure it out as they grew up – if they wanted to.

I had a yearning for something, but it wasn't until years later that I read Romans 1:19-20 and learned that God *has* planted in us a desire to know Him.

THE MAGIC KINGDOM

As a child, huge homes, grand yearly vacations, or designer anything were not part of my neighborhood or life, at least as far as I knew it. I'll never forget one day in 1955, driving with my family up the coast. All my brother and I knew was that it was a surprise.

We drove north for ninety minutes past Del Mar, Oceanside, the Marine Base at Camp Pendleton, and into Orange County, passing orange grove after orange grove. Through the breaks in the trees, we saw remnants of camouflaged bunkers covered in grassy sod, large fields surrounded by double fencing, and stockpiles of munitions. Some looked like torpedoes, deactivated but reminiscent of WWII. I remember my grandmother talking about complete blackouts along the Southern California coast as Japanese submarines patrolled our shoreline. During the drive from San Diego to Orange County, we passed hundreds of working small oil wells. They reminded me of giant woodpeckers bobbing up and down, beaks driving deep into the ground.

Finally, after many miles, we reached our destination – Disneyland!

In 1953, Walt Disney purchased a 160-acre orange grove in rural Anaheim with a vision of a magical kingdom. Two years later, in July of 1955, he opened the gates on a sweltering 101-degree day. There were eighteen rides and attractions. Just one month after its initial opening, my brother's and my dreams came true as we drove onto the property of Disneyland for the first time.

Our whole family walked around Main Street U.S.A., amazed at the colorful and whimsical shops, the horse-drawn carriages, the spotless streets, and the fanciful Disney characters waiting to welcome us. We had a family photo taken where we dressed like cowboys and saloon girls from the Wild West. We wandered in and out of every single store on Main Street. Mom and Dad bought me the most beautiful four-inch castle made from hand-blown glass. It had pink touches on top of the bubbly little towers.

Leaving Main Street, we headed toward Fantasyland, where Sleeping Beauty's Castle soared ahead of us. My brother and I hurried through the castle archway, unprepared for all the rides that awaited us. Each step around every corner left me in wide-eyed wonder. I was in awe of this new, enchanted fairytale kingdom, where all my dreams could come true.

Over the next few years, we repeated this drive many times and made many more memories at Disneyland. Our days always began in the massive parking lots where attractive trolleys picked up overly excited families and deposited them at the beautifully landscaped entrance to The Magic Kingdom. For those who just wanted to stroll around and enjoy a beautiful day, as many adults did, the entry fee was $1.00. To ride the attractions, additional ticket books were sold.

Each book featured a set amount of A tickets for rides on Main Street; B tickets for Tomorrowland; C tickets for the Teacups, Mr. Toad's Wild Ride, and Peter Pan; and D tickets – my favorite – for Tom Sawyer's Island. When the Matterhorn opened in 1959, it was originally a D ticket. However, it soon became part of the coveted E ticket, along with the Jungle Cruise (1955), Submarine Voyage (1959), It's a Small World (1966), Pirates of the Caribbean (1967), and the Haunted Mansion (1969). "It's an E-ticket ride!" became a popular phrase to describe anything exciting and awesome. My brother and I had a drawer full of leftover A and B tickets. Space Mountain didn't open until years later in 1977. In 1982, the ticket books were replaced with a general admission price.

After our initial visit, we went to Disneyland at least two to three times each year. I knew where every drinking fountain and bathroom was throughout the park. Disneyland was in the middle of a normal neighborhood, surrounded by small motels with small swimming pools. Even though we were only ninety minutes from home, we often stretched it into a two-day adventure, checking into one of these motels for the night. After a fun morning at Disneyland, we'd get our hands stamped to reenter the park later, leave around lunchtime, and head to our motel for an afternoon swim or a nap before returning to paradise around 4:00 p.m. At dusk, Disneyland's twinkly lights turned on to outline every building and ride. I thought it was fairies and lightning bugs – I just knew they lived in every tree! Later, we hurried to get the best spot on Main Street for the 9:00 p.m. parade. For us, this was a family vacation. I loved our time together. Disneyland, the small pool, and our motel room created wonderful memories!

As amazing as it was, the allure and wonder of Disneyland became less intriguing as my interest in boys took over my life.

SUMMER IN THE EARLY '60S

As I approached my tweens, I could not tell the truth. To this day, I honestly don't know why I chose to lie. Mom or Dad would ask me if I was over at a friend's house and I'd lie, telling them I was at the store or vice-versa. No matter how simple or mundane the question, I responded with a lie.

Often, this type of behavior in young children means they are testing their boundaries. I now know that sin nature is deeply embedded in each of us. Little toddlers steal, pinch, bite, and shove. As I grew older, I had no real reason to lie, but still, I continued. Because I was living in a godless void with little direction, I had no reason to seek change.

Parents have the awesome responsibility of molding and shaping little human beings into productive big human beings who leave the nest, hopefully. Most parents want to know who their child is hanging out with and what the other family's beliefs and expectations are, but my parents didn't. Maybe they didn't have any cares or expectations of their own, but for whatever reason, they never knew any of my friends' parents. There was never any discussion as to where I was going, what I was doing, or whether it was right or wrong.

Eventually, however, my lying caught up with me and I did get in trouble.

My years in sixth and seventh grades were a constant back and forth – two weeks on restriction, two weeks off, two weeks on, two weeks off. I sincerely think my parents had no clue what to do with me. Threats of being sent away to a private Catholic boarding school for girls was often thrown out in conversations.

They won't really send me away, will they?

The thought occasionally crept into my brain, but it still didn't curb my attitude or actions.

Famed vacation spots that I so casually took for granted were part of my normal life, like the town of Coronado. In the early '60s, Coronado only could be reached either by taking the ferry across San Diego Harbor or by driving the long route around the bay. This drive extended south of my hometown of Chula Vista, west to Imperial Beach (the most southwestern beach in the U.S.), and back north along a narrow strip of land called the Silver Strand, enclosed by the San Diego Bay on one side and the glistening Pacific Ocean on the other. It wasn't until the construction of the San Diego–Coronado Bay Bridge in February of 1967 that the isolated, magnificent, quaint town of Coronado gained freeway access. The town was brimming with Navy officers stationed at North Island Naval Air Station. Ocean-front mansions with separate maids' quarters lined the streets.

The jewel of Coronado was The Hotel Del Coronado, a historical treasure built on a peninsula. It was a huge, white, wooden Victorian hotel built in the 1880s. It had a bright red roof. This place was famous with presidents, royalty, and celebrities, and it was just a short walk from where my girlfriends and I went to the beach.

On a normal summer day, I went to the beach with three friends from my neighborhood. We piled into either my mom's red Volvo or the neighbor's station wagon. The Volvo looked like an oversized VW beetle, and my long surfboard hung off the roof rack, over both the hood and the trunk of the car. The neighbor's station wagon had rear seats that faced backwards, allowing us to roll the entire back window down to wave at the cars coming toward us – so cool! Sadly, the exhaust fumes funneled right through the open window, so being cool lasted all of about three minutes.

After summer school got out at noon every day, we packed up our bologna and cheese sandwiches (made with stick-to-the-roof-of-your-mouth Wonder Bread), baby oil mixed with iodine for our tans, zinc oxide cream for our noses, and beach towels. Our parents drove us the twenty minutes up The Silver Strand to Coronado. They dropped us off at about 12:30 p.m. and returned at 4:30 p.m. All summer long, we had four-hour stretches at the beach with no parental eyes.

The Coronado beach is extremely wide, so dragging my heavy six-foot bright red surfboard was a laborious chore. We plopped close to the lifeguard towers, mainly because the lifeguards were so cute, but also as a point of reference as to where we laid down our towels. We loved the music they blasted from the towers, like "Wipe Out," "Surfer Girl," "Surfin' U.S.A.," and "Surf City."

Once we arrived, I began the ritual of waxing my surfboard to make its fiber-glass coating non-slippery. A byproduct of the wax was surfer knots that devel-oped on my knees – an impressive surfer thing to have. Surfers had cool names like Gidget, Miki, Dewey, Great Kahuna, and Moondoggie. Mine was Pineapple.

The Pacific Ocean was not a nice ocean. By August, the ocean temperature rose all the way up to seventy degrees. Seventy-two was considered a heat wave, and no one wore wetsuits! Most of the time, my friends and I body surfed. The cold, rough swells and strong current carried us down the shoreline away from our towels, toward the Hotel Del Coronado.

My girlfriends and I got out of the ocean and walked freely all over the hotel grounds with sandy feet and wet bathing suits. Only a wrought iron fence with a gate separated the beach from the large saltwater pool. There were no locks, no security guards, and no guest ID badges. We routinely strolled past the outdoor cabana and walked around the bottom floor of the grand hotel, looking at all the luxurious store windows full of diamonds, pearl necklaces, beautiful broad-brimmed beach hats, magnificent shoes, and dresses to match. The men's stores were equally dapper. While perusing the store windows was exciting, our main goal was always the same – to find Kate.

No one ever stopped us. We wound our way up to the top floor, hoping to get a glimpse of Kate from an open bedroom door as the maids prepared a room for the next guest, but we never saw her. As twelve-year-old girls, the only thing we knew about Kate was that she was a ghost.

I later learned that Kate Morgan checked into the hotel on November 24, 1892 and was never seen alive again. While supposedly waiting for her lover to return, she was found in an exterior stairwell with a gunshot wound to the head. Her death was officially listed as a suicide, but why was she in the stairwell, and where was her lover? Kate is still the resident ghost of the Hotel Del Coronado. We looked for her almost every day, and every day I lied to my parents about what I did for four hours.

Before long, I abandoned my searches for Kate and started sneaking out with boys. I met them at the beach, left my surfboard, and walked the opposite direction of The Del. We'd spend the hours making out, as we called it. It became a problem when I returned late in the afternoon to my surfboard with a boy, and one of the parents would be waiting. I learned to lie not just to my parents, but to other parents as well.

Dad made a new rule – if I wanted to go surfing, I had to go to church. He never went to church, nor did Mom, but I was supposed to somehow find a church and go, just like that. I tried to finagle a deal and listen to some church service on the radio, but he wouldn't buy it. I had to physically go to a church.

The only family I knew who went to church was the one across the street, my second home where I had my nightly 6:00 p.m. dinners. They belonged to St. Pius X Catholic Church down the street from our liquor store, so I started going with them.

The services were still in Latin at that time, so I never paid any attention to the priests walking down the aisle, swinging their silver thuribles on chains with smoldering incense, sending pungent puffs of smoke wafting around the room. My girlfriend and I, both being boy crazy, passed the time by writing the names of whomever we were newly in love with.

Mrs. Tommy King, Mrs. Thomas King, Mr. and Mrs. Thomas King, Mrs. Sandee King.

The next month it would be Mrs. James Monroe, Mrs. Joe Shmoo, and so on. These dreamy fantasies were spawned on by all the kissing I had already been doing on the beach.

When my mom and dad went out, I started sneaking boys into the house. I now realize how stupid and gullible I was. I thought the boys really liked me. We'd kiss and they told me they loved me. But now I see that they really just loved the liquor from the Square Bottle.

Dad had a cabinet full of our square bottles in our home. The labels were removed and replaced with a single beautiful three-inch gold letter – G for gin, S for scotch, V for vodka, B for bourbon, and R for rum. Starting when I turned twelve, Mom and Dad went out every Friday night.

My girlfriends and I waited for their car to drive away. Then, the boys showed up and the party began. The square bottles came out of the cupboard, and we marked the level of the liquor with a pencil on the side of the bottle. After drinking Dad's booze, we filled it back up with water to the pencil line. My dad knew his liquor, yet he never said a word. He had to know how watered down it was. Again, I think they had no clue what to do with me.

I craved my father's attention. I wanted to be confronted. I would have loved for him to say, "Sandee what are you doing? Why? What can we do to help you understand how much we love you and want the best for you?" But it never happened.

Not only was I sneaking boys into the house, but I was also sneaking out of my bedroom window. I often met the current boyfriend at 2:00 a.m., complete with sleeping bags. Today, it is unthinkable to me to wander a neighborhood in the middle of the night. I snuck around in the total darkness, peering into people's homes and avoiding the headlights of cars. I hid behind bushes in shadows that hid me completely. I became carelessly comfortable prowling about in the wee hours. I lost my virginity somewhere between the age of twelve and thirteen. He said he loved me.

Girls often lose their virginity so early, and my heart aches for these young girls as they try to fill the void in their hearts. I know I kept trying to fill my own emptiness as boy after boy said he loved me. During this time, I constantly lied to cover up all my clandestine and immoral activities.

I wonder what would have stopped me from losing my virginity.

My parents? Peer pressure? Teaching me from an early age how special I was, that I was strong and needed to believe in myself? Belief that my daddy would protect me no matter what?

Belief in God?

Perhaps, and I would have had a far greater chance of avoiding the pain of feeling used, looking for the next boyfriend to love me.

I was only twelve.

I was searching.

Letters from private schools began arriving in the mail. My parents couldn't possibly be serious!

THE PONDEROSA AND MATT DILLON

Television was a focal point in our family. It literally brought us together, specifically on Tuesday and Sunday nights. Dad sat in his chair, Mom in hers, and I piled up pillows directly in front of the TV.

On Tuesdays, we started with the comedy *The Red Skelton Show*, moved to *Gunsmoke*, and finished with more laughter with *The Carol Burnett Show*. On Sunday evenings, we watched *Bonanza* followed by Rowan and Martin's *Laugh-In*, starring Goldie Hawn. Oh my gosh, it didn't get better than extraordinary comedy and good Westerns!

The three of us uproariously laughed at the slapstick skits, often laced with undertones of hilarious sexuality. On *The Carol Burnett Show*, the likes of Tim Conway and Harvey Korman tried desperately to keep straight faces but often turned aside to hold it together. The sexual jokes and gags on *Laugh In* were blatant. Other shows like *The Dean Martin Show* and *Johnny Carson* were full of excessive drinking, sexual innuendos, and flagrant flirtatious mannerisms with female guests. In the mid '60s and into the '70s, sexual humor, smoking, and gin martinis were the norm on TV.

In contrast, *Gunsmoke* and *Bonanza* portrayed men with the highest moral character. On *Gunsmoke*, Matt Dillon, the upright staunch law-abiding U.S. Marshal of Dodge City in the 1870s, played alongside Kitty, the owner of the Long Branch Saloon. No one really knew the extent of their relationship, but they appeared to be devoted to each other and had a mutual deep respect. He always protected her and stood up for what was right.

On Sunday night's *Bonanza*, we tuned into the happenings of the Ben Cartwright family. What a family! A widowed dad, his three adult sons, and a Chinese cook named Hop Sing lived on a vast ranch called The Ponderosa in the foothills of the Sierra Mountains. The boys occasionally wandered into Virginia City, a town on the Nevada side of the Sierras, east of Lake Tahoe. In the saloon, the ladies attempted to get their attention. The dad was the epitome of righteousness, constantly mentoring his adult boys. He guided them into doing what was right, even if it cost them their time and their money. Whatever the situation and ensuing discipline, it instilled the boys with a great deal of humility. The strength of Ben Cartwright was majestic to me. I longed for that kind of discipline, and also for the romance of Matt and Kitty.

Both Ben Cartwright and Matt Dillon represented strength in manhood, a proper guide for relationships and for how dads should treat their children. They took the role of protector – one for a woman, the other for his rambunctious sons.

I later realized I longed for the strength of a man, one who would tell me he loved me, who treasured and protected me, and who never used me. At the time, I had no idea that true love is rooted in Jesus. I didn't know who Jesus was.

THE UNTHINKABLE

Visiting the cousins on my mom's side of the family became a frequent activity for me when my uncle, a captain for Trans World Airlines, was transferred from Chicago to San Francisco. (In 2001, TWA was acquired by American Airlines.) Since they now lived in California, I visited them a great deal during the summers.

My uncle began flying when stewardesses had to be nurses and ladies wore hats, two-piece suits, and gloves. My aunt always brought back the menus from her first-class flights to exotic places. My uncle flew to the Far East, and his schedule was two weeks on and two weeks off. Every time he returned home from his ten-to-fourteen-day trips, he shared his stories with us. The glamour, the flight schedule, and the attraction of being a stewardess – their ability to travel and live comfortably in different cities – all began to take root in my soul. I became infatuated with the idea of being a stewardess.

My uncle, aunt, and cousins lived east of the San Francisco Bay area on Mount Diablo, outside of Walnut Creek. Numerous pilots and their families lived in this equestrian community. My cousins had horses and we'd ride freely for hours through fields that gleamed of golden wheat, unrestrained by fences or barbed wire. We then returned, settled the horses in for the day, and dove into their beautiful pool. In my view, the lifestyle of an airline captain was truly wonderful.

In 1962 – the summer between sixth and seventh grades – I returned home from a two-week visit with my cousins. My head was filled with dreams of marrying an airline captain.

Much to my dismay, Mom and Dad informed me that in the fall I would be attending The Convent of the Sacred Heart in El Cajon, a boarding school in the foothills east of San Diego. It was a very proper school.

After Labor Day, Mom and I purchased my sheets, blankets, school supplies, and uniforms, complete with black and white Oxford saddle shoes. I was angry – furious, actually – to be leaving whatever current boyfriend I had. This had all been pre-arranged. The day arrived for Mom and Dad to drop me off, and they already knew their way around the school and the location of my dorm room. Memories surfaced of visiting my brother's middle school military dorm room years earlier. It's interesting how we were both treated the same way by my parents.

The newly built dorm was bright, clean, fresh, and stark. Long, straight, glistening hallways stretched toward bright red exit signs at each end of the hall. Each room was totally self-contained, as wide as a twin bed plus about five feet. The long wall opposite the twin bed had a beautiful light-wood finish complete with built-ins – drawers, a fold-down desk and closet, and a chair. That was it.

Other girls decorated their rooms with posters, curtains, and pillows that matched their bedspreads for a cozy look and feel. My room remained painfully stark with very few of my personal belongings. I had no intentions of staying.

Fortunately, each room had a large window. Mine looked out on a courtyard and across to another dorm just like mine. After lights out, I sat at my open window and lit up a cigarette. I saw the glow of cigarettes from many other windows. From my perspective, everyone I saw on television as well as my parents and their friends smoked. It was portrayed as romantic and the thing adults do, especially after sex. The Marlboro Man was extremely handsome, rugged, and macho. At that time, we didn't yet know the dangers of tobacco, Vietnam wasn't really a war, and JFK was still alive. Society was still innocent. I wasn't.

My new inconceivable life at this Catholic school began early with chapel. We marched up the hill at 6:30 a.m., and a priest conducted the daily morning service. Everyone kneeled to make the sign of the cross, so I mimicked them. At the end of the first week, we rose from the pews and walked up the aisle in a line to the front of the chapel. What was going on? I watched, and I saw the priest mumbling something over each girl while he waved a white round flat piece of something in front of their face. Each girl then stuck out her tongue, and he placed the thin white thing there. When it was my turn, I just stood there and stuck my tongue out. Oh, my word, my first communion and I had no clue what in the world was happening. Imagine what I thought when I stepped into the booth for my first confession!

My years of going to my friend's Catholic church truly taught me nothing. The nuns at the school knew I wasn't Catholic, so there were no expectations. I'm sure they didn't think I would walk forward for communion. But still, not knowing anything about the Catholic faith plus my anger for being forced to be there equaled a spoiled, obnoxious, and extremely disrespectful girl.

After chapel, we marched down the hill to the dining hall for a lovely breakfast before heading off to our classes. Everything truly was done in a tasteful and refined manner. Our day consisted of classes, lunch, more classes, catechism, some sort of outdoor gym class, and a few treasured hours of free time before dinner.

Each evening, the tables were covered in white linens with matching napkins. The silverware was set out with soup and dinner spoons, salad and dinner forks, dessert forks, and butter and dinner knives. The Convent of the Sacred Heart was where I first learned how to properly eat an artichoke. Unbeknownst to me at the time, this was a Catholic finishing school for the finest ladies in San Diego. Most attendees would go on to the finest colleges, join the proper sororities, and marry the "right person." Little did I know how far that was from my future. Through the filter of my rebellious heart, I could not appreciate this place.

After dinner, it was time for homework, lights out, and my nightly cigarette.

After the first Friday of school, I went home for a visit. I managed to talk my parents into removing me from catechism class. From my second week of school forward, I went to the study hall instead.

A routine emerged. Monday through Friday consisted of the daily routine of school. On Friday afternoon, Mom or Dad picked me up. I was so happy to see them because it meant that in a few hours I would be at the Friday night high school football game with my friends. On Saturday, I went to the movies or played cards with my parents and their friends. On Sunday afternoon, I prepared to head back to school. I punished my parents with my sullenness and silence on the ride back to the Convent. There were times when I didn't say a word during the entire thirty-minute drive. Upon arrival, I slammed the car door behind me as I walked back into the dorm. I must have caused my parents a great deal of pain.

The nuns were incredibly sweet. The students were their life, and, if I had cared, I might have been able to understand that. They all wore long black habits with modest head pieces consisting of two-inch white bands and black veils covering the back of their necks. The Mother Superior wore a heavily starched white cornette that looked like wings on each side of her head. This was before Sally Field and *The Flying Nun*, but that's what the Mother Superior looked like.

My resentment and inability to fit in drew the attention of the Mother Superior. One January day, she asked me to join her for a walk. We strolled the perimeter of campus, her hands folded inside her habit sleeves.

"Are you happy at the convent?"

"No," I responded, curtly.

"Why not?"

"Because the dorms remind me of a whore house!"

She responded calmly.

"I see."

We walked in silence the rest of the way.

How in the world did I come up with that response? Truthfully, it was straight out of *Gunsmoke* – the red exit lights at the end of the hall, my room with only a bed and a chair, and an active imagination of what might have occurred upstairs in the Long Branch Saloon created the picture for me.

I was asked to leave, only lasting one semester at The Convent of the Sacred Heart.

Back at home, things started to change. I became more responsible and grew up a bit. My room was clean, and my grades improved greatly. I certainly can't attribute that to anything more than my motivation to become a stewardess and marry my airline captain. Perhaps it was the nuns praying for me.

On Saturday nights, the Chula Vista Community Center hosted dances or battles of the bands that drew in all the high school students. For the first few weeks back at home, I bought a new skirt for each of the dances. Soon, Mom and Dad told me they couldn't afford to pay for a new skirt every weekend. Instead, they bought a sewing machine. Voila! I became a seamstress overnight. This continued and grew into a passion; I loved sewing my own clothes. By my senior year, I made the majority of my clothes, including my dress to the senior prom. My domesticity flowed over to the kitchen as well, earning me a Betty Crocker $25.00 scholarship. At the time, the average price of gas was thirty-three cents a gallon and the average income was $7,300 per year. Twenty-five bucks was a decent scholarship. It's impossible to imagine that type of award in today's world!

TIJUANA AND HIGH SCHOOL

As I became more responsible, my rudeness to my parents vanished along with lying, probably because they quit asking me questions. Dad, with a grin on his face, occasionally asked me for a cigarette if he ran out. He must have thought that bonded us. One thing that didn't change was my need to feel loved; I never spent a day without a boyfriend or a weekend without drinking Dad's liquor.

In high school, I found a new way to get to Tijuana – the fake ID.

The legal age to cross the border without parents was eighteen. By my junior year of high school, a group of us went to Tijuana on a regular basis. Sometimes we parked our car on the American side, walked across, and got a taxi to Revolución Boulevard. Other times, we actually drove across the border, parked, and hit the bars. I even took my mom's car a few times.

Our goal was to get drunk and disco dance. We all adhered to a set plan, a kind of "how to" blueprint for a successful night of getting wasted. We started at the Hotel Nelson with our first beer, then we walked across the street to the bowling alley. I have no clue why it was called "the bowling alley" because there was no bowling. It was just a bar that served the most amazing shredded beef (at least I think it was beef) burritos. We all ate one to fill our stomachs so we could drink more. We learned quickly not to drink on an empty stomach.

Our next stop was The Long Bar for a few more beers – usually stale, warm, and flat. We knew of places called the Green Door and the Blue Note (or was it the Green Note and the Blue Door?) where rumor had it that so-called "donkey shows" took place. None of us ever spoke of them and we heard later the rumors were not true, sort of. Even to me, a person with very few moral beliefs, this type of depravity was beyond my comprehension. Sadly, I had no concern for the women involved. I just thought it was sick and disgusting. I guess I figured if they did it, they liked and wanted it. I hadn't heard of sex trafficking.

Our last stop was disco dancing at the Aloha Club, where we switched to Tequila Sunrises or Slow Gin Fizzes. It was always overcrowded with little air circulating, the beat deafening, and the mirrored disco ball twirling from the ceiling.

After an hour of dancing and drinking, the smell that began to permeate from the place was a putrid combination of perspiration, vomit, pee, and English Leather or Jade East cologne. We actually had to walk out a side door and into an alley to find the bathroom. We were so dumb, stupid, and naïve. So many things could've happened to us. Someone could have slipped drugs into our drinks, stolen our money, stolen our car keys, or worse.

Most of us had a curfew of 12:30 a.m., so we gathered around 11:00. We still had to face the guards at the border, get across, and drive home on the busy interstate. Food made it easier for us to walk straight and attempt to get sober, so we always stopped at a street vendor's cart. Everyone grabbed a *torta*, a bun filled with seasoned meat. We never questioned what we were eating; it was probably better that way, and the tequila and gin sterilized it anyway. We never got sick, and the tortas were delicious every time.

We worked our way back to the border. As we got closer, traffic grew heavier and slowly came to a stop. Cars spread out over ten or so lanes, and we waited our turn.

As cars inched their way up to the gates, small children, often barefoot, walked up and down the rows with the most sorrowful eyes, hoping people would buy gum or let them wash the car windshield for tips. Along with the children, elderly bent-over women displayed velvet paintings with faces of Elvis, the crucified Christ, or Aztec warriors carrying half-naked women up mountains to be sacrificed. It was close to midnight and these little boys and girls and the elderly were trying desperately to earn a living, yet we laughed and brushed them off, trying not to make eye contact. I never thought about how or where they lived. I simply saw them as a nuisance.

Whether we crossed the border by foot, taxi, or in a private car, the questions were always the same.

"Where were you born?"

"San Diego."

"What was the purpose of your visit?"

"Dinner."

"Are you bringing anything back?"

"No."

"Thank you."

We were always waved through.

Occasionally, a car in front of us was stopped. Sometimes it was obvious that a guard had been tipped off to look for a particular car, motioning it over for a strip search. The guards opened the trunk, pulled up the floor mats, and searched the back seat. Sometimes the seats themselves were pulled out or the side doors were pulled off. Ceiling upholstery was slashed open and carpets were pulled up to reveal false floors. We watched as the driver and passengers were hauled off. It never dawned on us that we were in the presence of true danger, drugs, and evil.

Car after car of drunk teenagers slowly exited the Mexico-United States Border crossing, easing their way into the next dangerous challenge – driving home on Interstate 5, the main interstate on the West Coast of the United States. It runs from Tijuana all the way to Canada. Considering we were entering an extremely busy freeway from the busiest border crossing, it was truly a miracle we never killed anyone.

Whoever was driving was definitely drunk along with all the other drivers returning from Tijuana. If we could supernaturally look back at those nights, I believe we would see God's mighty warriors literally standing on the white lines, magnificent wings outstretched, prohibiting cars from getting close to each other. I can only recall ever losing one friend; he went off a cliff by Rosarita Beach, south of Tijuana. I truly believed God protected the rest of us. There is no other answer for our safe return week after week.

When I arrived home, Mom pretended to be up watching a late-night movie. In reality, she must have been holding her breath with a knot in the pit of her stomach, waiting for me to walk through the door. She always acted nonchalant, but I know she must have been worried. I'm sure she knew I'd been out drinking; my stench from The Aloha Club had to be a dead giveaway. Dad was sound asleep and snoring loudly.

Why didn't anyone stop me? No one asked why I was destroying my life. I crawled into bed after saying goodnight, avoiding the goodnight kiss, which would have validated my whereabouts even more. As I lay upon my bed, the room began to spin. Proverbs 23:34-35 described me perfectly; I was like a drunken sailor "who lies down in the midst of the sea, like one who lies on the top of a mast… When shall I awake? I must have another drink."

Tijuana was a depraved time in my life. How could I look into the eyes of girls so drunk or drugged that they'd never get back across the border or return home safely and not care? How could I look into the eyes of small children and the elderly and just turn away? Yet I could, and I did. My heart was cold, and I had little regard for myself. I continued to search for love in my next boyfriend.

Many teenage girls are self-absorbed and couldn't care less about anyone else. Compassion comes with trials, time, and age. But this was more than that. I was looking in the face of child slavery, sex trafficking, and discarded elderly people fending for themselves, and their plight was of no concern to me. These people returned to the Tijuana dump where they only had stinky cardboard boxes to call home. They lived in a literal trash dump, and the beautiful night lights of San Diego illuminated the coastline just twelve miles north.

I was still attempting to hang with the surfer crowd, so I often also snuck out of the house at 5:00 a.m., too. I grabbed my surfboard and met my buddies at La Jolla Shores. We were in the water by 5:30 a.m. I guess they'd heard there would be some great swells. I'm assuming my friends read some tidal reports, but I just followed the boys.

We paddled out, the water still black with the sun yet to rise. We paddled directly over The La Jolla Trench, an ominous, deep submarine canyon, home to many types of sharks including the Great White. Yet, there I was as the day was dawning with my legs dangling over the side of my board, ready to ride a wave. Ha! I was so pathetic. I caught maybe five waves during my entire surfing career.

After the sun came up, we hurried back to the parking lot, strapped our boards onto the car, and headed to Chula Vista. These were school mornings, so I had to sneak back home and jump in the shower before Mom and Dad woke up at 7:30. These mornings had nothing to do with my love of surfing. They were born from my desire to keep the current boyfriend and the trips to Tijuana.

THE COLLEGE LIFE

The time came to start looking at colleges. Most of my friends were planning to go to the local junior college and then transfer to San Diego State after two years. In the mid-to-late '60s, attending a four-year college was not expected, especially for girls. For guys, going to trade schools and becoming electricians or plumbers was encouraged. Getting married right out of high school was not uncommon.

I decided I wanted to become a physical education teacher. I had always been a bit of a jock, interested in anything that kept me outdoors. I also wanted to be one of the few that escaped my hometown. Deep down, I felt tarnished by my damaged reputation fueled by stories about how I slept around. I knew I wouldn't fit in at the local junior college or in the sorority scene, so the best thing to do was leave. This began a long series in my life of packing up and leaving.

I actually graduated from Hilltop High School in 1967 with a B average, so I had high hopes of being accepted to a college away from home. I applied to San Jose State in Northern California, Arizona State University in Phoenix, and Northern Arizona University in Flagstaff. I was accepted to all three. I felt that the wisest choice to make was to head to Northern Arizona University because they offered snow skiing for credit! Flagstaff sits at 7,000 feet and the San Francisco Peaks are just ten minutes away, rising to 12,633 feet. I didn't know how to snow ski, but it seemed like a great idea.

The boyfriend I had the summer before college had an unusual philosophy. He wanted to prepare me for college and make sure I could take care of myself. We accomplished this by going to Tijuana several nights a week to build my stamina for drinking. He said boys would try to take advantage of me by getting me drunk, so he wanted me to be able to drink them under the table. How sweet.

I started NAU with a clean slate. No one knew of my past. Still, things didn't really change. Deep inside, I was the same girl longing for the supportive love that only God can give us. I still had no morals, no parameters, no boundaries, no internal compass to rely on. I was like a reed swaying in the breeze; whatever came along was cool. If a person wanted to believe in something, it was fine, no matter what it was. Actually, I actually admired when people had opinions of their own because I had none.

To no surprise, I hung with a group of heavy drinkers and smokers who were sexually promiscuous, hardly different than what I left behind. I had a new boyfriend, both of us far away from home. Of course, I was in love.

Fortunately, my night life was controlled by the House Mother. Yes, we had a curfew, and each female dorm had an older woman who lived in a small apartment on the main floor. She locked the doors at one minute past curfew. I loved it! I had restrictions, parameters that had to be met, and a reason why I had to stop doing what I was doing and get back home. That curfew provided me with a great deal of comfort in a world where, as college students, we were free to do as we pleased.

College was one of the few times in my life that I enjoyed the company of other girls without guys around. We had the freedom to just be silly. We had water fights, mud facials, and, of course, lots of boy talk. I felt secure behind the locked doors of my all-girls dorm.

On a national level, drugs had taken over. Professor Timothy Leary proclaimed that LSD was the way to open up the mind. His mantra to his students was "turn on, tune in, and drop out." Parties were full of LSD-spiked punch and marijuana-filled brownies. In the background, Jimi Hendrix sang "Purple Haze" with all its psychedelic glory. The Beatles sang "Lucy in the Sky with Diamonds," "Yellow Submarine," and "Sgt. Pepper's Lonely Hearts Club Band." Hippies took over parts of the Haight-Ashbury in San Francisco with their tie-dye, acid, flower power, peace-brother-love, hate of the Vietnam war, and overwhelming smell of patchouli oil. Somehow, I avoided all the drugs and hate patchouli oil to this day!

I had many friends who got lost in this drug-fogged world, literally and figuratively. Some actually went to San Francisco in search of this Leary lifestyle, while others just indulged where they were. Either way, their minds were gone.

I vividly recall the night I took one puff of weed (or grass or whatever the popular name was at the time for marijuana). It was my first semester at NAU. We were all drinking beer.

"Hey, let's go in the back room," someone said.

Of course, I followed. The acrid smell hit me, and then someone offered me a drag. I took one, but that was it. For the first time, I walked out of a place, not caring what anyone thought of me. Somewhere in me I did have a backbone. I still went through a carton of cigarettes a week and drank hard liquor and beer, but my odd sense of morality drew a line in the sand against drugs.

During that first semester, I don't remember studying or any of the classes I took, and my grades showed it. Right before Christmas, a massive snowstorm hit Flagstaff. The snowstorm of 1967 is in the record books as the most severe snow event ever to hit Northern Arizona. For nine straight days, December 12-20, eighty-six inches of snow dumped on the city. The Navajo Nation, a close neighbor of Flagstaff, was devastated. Many people were trapped in their homes without power and supplies for more than ten days. Temperatures dropped to six below zero. Thirty-two people died due to starvation or lack of supplies while hiking through the snow in search of help.

Seven feet of snow fell on the campus. We dug out tunnels to walk through, walls of snow rising on each side. The President of the University urged students to leave as soon as possible or be trapped at school for the holidays. The Amtrak train paralleled historic Route 66, both flowing straight through the center of Flagstaff. Most of us took the Amtrak to Los Angeles since cars were already buried under feet of snow and parents couldn't get through.

After a short visit at home for Christmas (including a few trips to Tijuana), I took the Amtrak back to Flagstaff. I arrived on campus in early January where I was greeted by massive icicles hanging from the roof of my three-story dorm. These icicles, fifteen feet long and two feet wide, were deadly if broken loose. The snow didn't melt for months, and the road up to the mountain remained blocked. That meant no snow skiing credits for me. I didn't have enough credits to become a sophomore the following year, either.

I came to a self-sacrificing conclusion – I was wasting my parent's money while living a promiscuous lifestyle, drinking and not studying. Returning to school would be foolish. I felt like this was such an honorable choice, but this decision fed into the ongoing pattern I'd established with my parents. As long as something made me happy, it was fine to quit.

Even after my heroic decision to quit school, I thought nothing of my reckless way of living. My destructive patterns continued. I never let the hurt from a break-up last long enough to feel pain or remorse. I always had the next first date within days of leaving the last love of my life.

CHICKEN PLUCKER

After quitting college, it was easy for my brother to talk me into buying a really cute red Fiat Spyder two-seater convertible.

Now that I had a car, I needed a job to afford the car. My brother and his family lived in Orange County. He was the manager of an Alpha Beta, a defunct chain grocery store in Southern California. I got a job at the main Alpha Beta warehouse and moved in with my brother, his wife, and my nephew.

My first job on the assembly line was…a chicken plucker!

I inspected whole chickens that were destined for the in-store rotisseries. As the chickens passed by, I quickly plucked off any remaining feathers and quills, then tucked the legs and wings back into the twine that held them in place. Due to the fast monotonous rhythm of chicken after chicken, I quickly got the hang of it. If I made a mistake, chickens rolled off the end of the belt unchecked, feathers and quills still present. I knew I could be fired if too many chickens escaped my inspection.

After a while, I became confident in my quill and feather plucking ability and I started to talk with my fellow pluckers. The lady next to me was so sweet. She told me how she and her husband had eloped after their third date.

"Honey, when you know it's right, you just know."

They had been married for more than thirty years, the same length of time she had been working on the assembly line.

I left the house for work before sunrise, my car merging with thousands of others on the Los Angeles freeway. I never saw the light of day except on weekends. On the assembly line, I was always aware of the time clock. Lunch was allowed only in the break room, and supervisors were always watching production. I wanted sunshine and fresh air, but it was on the other side of the warehouse. It was too far to walk, and I couldn't waste my precious allotted time for lunch.

Living with my brother's family allowed me the chance to spend special time with my nephew. We had a blast in their community pool. My brother loved to pull pranks on me, and being part of his family was fun. However, I knew this wouldn't be home for long. I wanted to get out of the chicken-plucking business and go after my passion – becoming a stewardess.

My uncle had been a TWA captain for more than twenty-five years. He and his wife truly had a loving marriage, and I loved visiting them. They were devoted to each other. Since this devotion was absent in my home, seeing a husband and wife enjoy one another was wonderful for me.

While I was visiting them one weekend, my uncle mentioned TWA was hiring.

This was it!

My dream was going to come true. I was going to get out of the chicken-plucking business and embrace the life of being a stewardess. I wanted to fly international routes to Hong Kong, just like my uncle. I wanted to marry my captain and travel the world like my aunt. Then we would have children and live happily ever after.

I interviewed with TWA in the morning, at the Los Angeles Airport. In the afternoon, I interviewed with American Airlines.

"Sandee, you're a shoo-in," my uncle said. "They'll love you and hire you on the spot." Both airlines told a different story.

When I didn't get my dream job with either airline, I was shocked. I honestly don't even remember the interviews. What could I possibly have said or done or not done? Didn't they know I was perfect for this job? I had been hearing about my aunt and uncle's adventures my whole life. I was devastated. My dreams of flying internationally were gone.

By living with my brother's family, I saved up a little money to move back home to Chula Vista. I continued to pay for my car and gas. Then, I heard that a local airline, Pacific Southwest Airlines, was hiring. PSA was based in San Diego – a huge plus because I'd just started dating a really cute guy.

We'll call him *SS* for Strong and Sexy.

FLYING WITH PSA

In January of 1969, I had my one and only interview with Pacific Southwest Airlines. I was told to wear a miniskirt.

When I arrived at the hangar at the San Diego Airport, I entered a lobby full of other young women, all in miniskirts and extra-high heels. In the meeting room, three male interviewers sat behind an eight-foot table. We exchanged pleasantries and introductions, and I answered a few basic questions like where I'm from and what schools I'd attended.

After this, the real interview began.

"Sandee, would you please walk across the room and stand over there?"

The purpose of this was to look at my legs.

"Please come back this way and stand right here."

The two most important questions followed.

"Are you currently dating anyone?"

I answered no, of course, even though my newest boyfriend was awesome. It was common knowledge at the time that stews were single.

"Our training is extensive, and we invest a lot in it. Do you have any plans on getting married in the near future?"

"No," I answered again.

Bam, the interview was over. Within a few days, I would receive a call if I got the job.

I did receive a call with the job offer, with one stipulation – to lose weight. I was 5'6" and only weighed 134 pounds! I was instructed to drop ten and report mid-February for class.

On the first day, we received a massive three-ring binder, at least four inches thick. It was filled with material that our six-week training would cover – all the aircraft types, galley set-ups, serving procedures, emergency equipment, emergency evacuations (both water and land), and first aid and CPR. When I arrived home that first night, I was exhausted. Thoughts of *I can't do this!* screamed in my head as I stared at the volume of information. Even with all my doubt, I showed up to class the next day.

The instructors stressed that our primary function was the safety of our passengers. We had to know how to administer first aid and get them off the plane in an emergency. We had to be prepared for any type of situation; serving gin martinis was secondary. Our knowledge was tested along the way. We had to perform mock-up fire drills and pretend evacuations while adhering to all FAA guidelines and standards. My stewardess career was starting out to be less glamorous than I expected!

Our first Friday came to a close; I made it through week one! My weekend was spent studying and preparing for the next section of training.

After this first week, I started losing classmates. They were flunking out, feeling the intense pressure of how much we had to know, and realizing this job wasn't all just fun and glamour. For some, this just wasn't their cup of tea.

During the second week of training, we learned about emergency equipment. Every imaginable kind was in the classroom – water and carbon dioxide fire extinguishers, axes, flashlights, first aid kits, first aid vests, and seat cushions for floatation. We practiced with every piece of equipment over and over again.

During the third week, we learned all of the different types of PSA aircraft – Electra L-188, Boeing 727-100 and 200, and Boeing 737-200. We had to remember all the equipment for each type of craft and be able to run to it in seconds, all while wearing three-inch heels and a miniskirt.

By this time, we had mastered all of the portable emergency equipment, so our focus shifted to the emergency slide or life raft. For ground landings, we slung the door of the plane open, allowing the slide to fall out toward the ground. For water landings, we carried the slide to the over-wing exit area. It weighed close to forty pounds! Once the aircraft was floating, we opened the over-wing exit and threw the door out the window. We then heaved the slide through the window and inflated it on the wing. We directed the passengers safely out of the aircraft while keeping the slide from floating away.

During week four, we learned more about how to evacuate an airplane. We were taught to be in charge, forceful and strong. Passengers would be looking to us for direction, expecting us to save their lives. We learned the appropriate commands and how to yell them in an authoritative voice.

"BRACE, BRACE, HEADS DOWN, HEADS DOWN. UNFASTEN SEAT BELTS, UNFASTEN SEAT BELTS. COME THIS WAY, COME THIS WAY, LEAVE BELONGINGS BEHIND, LEAVE BELONGINGS BEHIND. JUMP, JUMP, GET AWAY FROM THE AIRCRAFT, GET AWAY FROM THE AIRCRAFT."

We learned how to size up passengers. We were trained to look for able-bodied men, ask if they'd be willing to help, and reseat them close to an exit. We explained what to do in case we were preoccupied – sort-of a crash course in Emergency Landing 101. During my career, I regularly looked for motorcycle-type guys to ask for assistance. They always answered, "Ma'am, if there's anything you need, we are here to help." They were always respectful and nice!

Week five was first aid training, which I hated. This section terrified me! Maybe I was fearful I'd do something wrong and make things worse. We focused on all the ailments a passenger may develop while on board – strokes, heart attacks, diabetic comas, epileptic seizures, shortness of breath, choking, and even delivering babies! We practiced CPR on each other, as the CPR dummy Annie wasn't created until years later. To this day, I still mentally block out this part of my training. (God must have known I might hurt someone. I never had a true first aid incident in my whole flying career!)

The last week of training was devoted to procedures like serving, storing or checking oversized bags, and locking down everything in the galley. During this week, we were also fitted for our uniforms – a celery green conservative dress with orange velvet trim on the jacket, orange ruffled pettipants underneath, orange knee-high boots, a pair of orange high heels (no flats were allowed until years later), an orange purse, and an orange triangle velvet hat, which rested at angle on our foreheads – très chic! When our one-year anniversary rolled around, we were able to trade our triangle hats for round velvet bouffants. We were issued an orange round suitcase for our overnight trips. This was before suitcases had wheels, and it looked like a giant hat box. My right shoulder and back ached for years from carrying it. Maybe that's why I now list to the right when I walk.

After our training was completed, we took a final exam and completed our administrative paperwork. Finally, graduation had arrived!

Graduation Day was on March 31, 1969. Our class had dwindled down to eighteen. The ceremony was at the Bahia Hotel on Mission Bay. Hugs, kisses, and delighted parents surrounded us, and the commencement speeches confirmed that we were the best class ever. My parents even received a letter of congratulations from our local Congressman Lionel Van Derlin. Our graduation date became everything; it was now my seniority number, and seniority ruled our world. That number determined which flights I received, my monthly bid, my vacation choices, and more. Annual raises were not based on merit but length of service. When I finally retired after twenty-eight years, I was number 337 out of about 11,000. If I could have sold my seniority number to the highest bidder, it would have greatly enhanced my retirement!

After graduation, we were required to shadow a senior stewardess for the next two weeks so we'd know what the job was really like. During those two weeks, we experienced every type of flight.

On early morning flights, we learned all about pre-flight checks on an airplane that had been sitting overnight. The first pre-flight of the day was always the most detail oriented. We walked through and checked the emergency equipment, notifying the senior stew when the job was complete. We then concentrated on the galley where we made coffee, got fresh ice, and restocked the liquor. Everything had to be ready for the day ahead.

Once all passengers were boarded, the cabin was secure, and the doors were closed, we began our inflight safety announcement. It was similar to what is heard today – how to fasten the seatbelt, how to evacuate an airplane, where the exits are located, and so on. During our two-week shadowing period, we were still very serious. However, over time, we added humor to get people's attention.

We did our final walk down the aisle as the aircraft taxied to take-off position. We ensured all tray tables were locked and luggage was stowed. I hadn't gained my air legs yet, so I felt like a drunken sailor. Walking in two-to-three-inch heels on a moving aircraft is difficult! After the walk-through, we sat in a passenger aisle seat. We weren't allowed to sit in a jump seat until our mentoring process was complete.

Once we were in the air, we served beverages on all flights regardless of how short the duration. Back then, we even served coffee and juice on the ten-minute flight between San Jose and Oakland! We had to prepare for service while the aircraft was still in a vertical position. Yanking a heavy beverage cart out of its braked and secured position and locking it sideways was quite the feat.

Early morning flights were easy compared to the rush of the afternoon and evening cocktail flights. The cocktail-hour flights started around noon. We began serving drinks on the ground while passengers boarded through the aft galley. After the routine luggage check and safety demonstration, we picked up any remaining cocktails as passengers raced to take their last gulp. We double-checked galley latches and got to our seats for take-off, usually as the aircraft was making its 180° turn onto the runway and revving up for takeoff.

Once in the air and still climbing, we pushed our massively heavy carts from the forward and aft galleys into the aisle to begin beverage service all over again. We sometimes had to do this twelve times a day for short hops up and down the California coastline.

As a flight was approaching its destination, the captain would signal us with three dings over the PA system as we descended through 10,000 feet. Technically, we should have been preparing the cabin for landing and sitting in our seats, but invariably we would still be in the aisles serving with galleys wide open and trash still to be picked up. We scrambled to get everything stowed, locked, and cleaned prior to touch down. We found ourselves barely getting strapped into our jump seats – or in my case, still a passenger seat – as the wheels touched down.

As a new kid on the block during this initiating period, I went home absolutely, totally exhausted. My feet felt permanently pinched from being confined to their stylish high-spiked heel prison. My entire body hurt from pushing heavy carts uphill, walking miles each day, and completing twelve to sixteen take-offs and landings.

Not only did everyone drink on these flights, everyone also smoked. So besides hurting at the end of the day, I reeked of cigarette smoke – every pore and every thread of my clothing stank (and still stank after being washed). I hung my clean uniforms in a separate hall closet so I wouldn't contaminate the rest of my clothes!

At the end of the two-week shadowing period, we had another final test. We were silently watched and monitored the entire day to make sure we knew how to do all the pre-flight, departure, landing, and deplaning responsibilities in our mile-high heels (while also properly flirting with the male passengers). By the end of the last day, we were ready to fly on our own.

Phew and hallelujah!

PRECIOUS STEWARDESS ASSOCIATION

Pacific Southwest Airlines began service in 1949 with weekly flights between the two Navy bases in San Diego and Oakland. It was locally dubbed as the Poor Sailor's Airline, and the inexpensive flights up and down the California coast required no seat reservations. By 1969, PSA had become the airline known for its fun, friendly, laid-back service and for its stewardesses. *Frequent Flyer Magazine* labeled PSA the original "coffee, tea, or me" airline.

In the late '60s, the job of stewardess was well-known for its glamour. And boy, was the glamour taken seriously!

In addition to all our other training, we knew that our looks were *very* important. Weigh-ins were part of our normal lives, as well as taking laxatives and water pills on the days before. We were instructed to wear false eyelashes and a padded bra (or they could recommend a doctor for enhancements). False nails were highly encouraged, and we were only allowed to wear Hula Orange lipstick by Revlon. Our nude panty hose was required to have a bit of a shimmer, and we had to carry at least one extra pair; runs were an absolute no-no.

Our hair had to be worn up and secured – absolutely no loose hairs flying about – or we could wear a wig. Us newbies still had to wear our triangle hats (signifying we were freshmen stewardesses), so we wore them at a jaunty angle. We then pulled our hair back and attached a hairpiece that covered the backs of our heads. We also had fashionable side curls that we glued to the sides of our faces!

About every two weeks, a group of us visited Tijuana to have our hair pieces styled. The stylist pinned them to a Styrofoam white head, combed out the curls, and smoothly arranged the large intertwined loopy rolls back into place. When finished, they sprayed hair lacquer over the whole thing. After a few drinks, we headed back to San Diego with our Styrofoam heads and hair pieces in the back seat. Between the lacquer and Crazy Glue holding down our side curls, our hair wouldn't move in a jet engine blast, or even a hurricane! I had two tiny perpetual red spots on each of my cheeks from the Crazy Glue.

When my one-year anniversary came, I traded in my triangle hat for a round orange velvet bouffant hat that covered the entire back of my head. This was fabulous! I was now able to dispense with the hair piece and just pull my hair up under my hat. I did still have my Crazy Glue side curls. Crazy Glue was a staple item in my purse for my hair, broken fingernails, and panty hose runs!

My stewardess class was fortunate and never had to be on reserve. I immediately began to bid for flights. Since I was at the bottom of the seniority list, I got the worst flights. I always worked late nights and weekends, but I was based in

San Diego. This worked for me as I was still dating my new boyfriend, SS. I found my first roommate, a girl who'd graduated in the class right behind mine, and we moved into a two-bedroom apartment east of Balboa Park on Redwood Street.

The commuter flights functioned like the freeway system in California, heavy in the morning and late afternoon. I recognized certain passengers who flew every day. For them, flying was the equivalent of getting into a car and driving to work each morning. The price of a ticket from San Diego to Los Angeles was $6.97, and Burbank to San Francisco was just $14.00! Most of the luggage on those flights were men's briefcases. Because our overhead racks were wide open back then, passengers were asked to place their luggage under the seat in front of them.

Now that I was out on my own, I often flew with the same stewardesses and flight crew. PSA was a small airline, and we soon felt like a family, recognizing each other and learning names. We started joking with each other and with passengers. It didn't take me long to realize that passengers were ignoring me during the safety demonstration, so I, along with many of my fellow stews, started incorporating some humor into our announcements. Since we often had days with sixteen take-offs and landings, we had to do something to bring a smile!

Many things were easier back then. We made jokes, we laughed, and security checks didn't exist. But some things were more difficult – like the smoking.

I loved my job, but cigarette smoke was one of the biggest downsides. Eventually, passengers started to demand a non-smoking section. Since PSA catered to smokers and drinkers, accommodating the few over the majority was a big decision.

The first non-smoking section was the first four rows on the left side of the aircraft. The twelve non-smoking passengers on the left side of the plane glared and exchanged snarky comments with the smoking passengers on the right side. Over time, the right side was added to the non-smoking section, along with other rows. If there were no seats left in the non-smoking section, they added rows – if a person in row fourteen wanted to be in the non-smoking section, rows one through fourteen became non-smoking. Finally, the smokers revolted and demanded they'd be guaranteed seats.

They ended up designating the last six rows as the smoking section. This made the aft cabin almost unbearable to work in. The stewardesses with the least seniority (like me) were stuck back there. One fresh air vent was in the galley, so we literally took a gulp of fresh cabin air before entering this smoking section and rushed back to the vent as soon as we could. Finally, we started rotating who worked back there so it would be fair.

I was still a smoker myself at the time, but one morning, I arrived home from a flight knowing I was coming down with the flu. My apartment smelled like a dirty ashtray. After many nauseated hours in front of the toilet, I never picked up a cigarette again.

Smoking is a huge cultural difference between that time and modern day; it's almost impossible to imagine a current airplane full of smoke! Another huge cultural difference between now and then is how we were expected to flirt with the men.

At the time, this was viewed as part of our job. Men often placed their brief-cases in the overhead rack just to watch us stretch up to retrieve them. They also liked to present us with a $100.00 bill for a $1.00 drink to watch us squirm and become flustered. They were probably hoping to get a free drink due to limited change. We found great joy when we could dig up ninety-nine $1.00 bills!

The flirty culture didn't exist just with the passengers; it extended to the crew, too. During training, they jokingly told us about two particular captains that would definitely flirt with us – if not more. We had to steer clear of those two! We called them Captain Jack (a little cuter than Captain Jack Sparrow) and Captain Kirk (way cuter than Captain Kirk on the Enterprise!).

Once, I returned from an overnight in San Francisco, arriving home at 8:00 a.m. I was looking forward to a quiet apartment. I knew my roommate had an early check-in and was already gone. However, I wasn't prepared for the surprise she left.

My roommate was *incredibly* messy, almost unbearably. She never washed a dish, always left the trash overflowing, and left her hair all over the bathroom. Even though I was happy to be home, I was prepared to walk into a filthy mess.

When I opened the door, I was shocked. The living room and kitchen were spotless. Completely puzzled, I walked past our clean bathroom, and then I heard a male voice from her bedroom.

"Hi there."

Walking in, I said, "Who are you?"

"I'm Captain Jack," he replied with a smirky grin.

He then offered to share the bed with me, and I declined. My roommate obviously had no concern leaving him behind.

I walked back into the kitchen and opened the cupboard under the sink where the trash can lived. All the trash she had stuffed in there poured out. I opened another cupboard and found all the dirty dishes she had hidden. The bathroom was the same; everything had been crammed under the sink. All cleaned up for Captain Jack.

When my roommate returned, she and I had a meeting. She found a new apartment. From then on, my boyfriend SS rarely went back to his place. I was in heaven with my man. We spent our free nights dancing at the Aloha Club in Tijuana. I felt safe in his arms as we swayed to the beat under the flashing disco ball. His aftershave (Was it Jade East?) covered up the sweaty smells of everyone else.

In 1966, a unique club began strictly to honor PSA's repeat customers. It all started with a particular stewardess noticing that she was saying hello and goodbye to the same men day after day, week after week. When recognition truly set in, she began to say, "Hello precious, nice to see you again." Some of the passengers started bringing her donuts and flowers. With her own money, she printed up certificates and membership cards, and the club was formed – The Precious Stewardess Association. It continued well into the '70s.

The club took on a life of its own, probably due to the friendly fun nature of PSA and the culture at the time. This was before jetways, hijackings, security checks, and non-smoking sections. Flights were full of liquor and very few women. Sexual innuendos while having a cocktail and cigarette were as commonplace as breathing. Many movies from that era will help explain how becoming a member of the Precious Stewardess Association was considered a prestigious thing.

The cards were highly coveted and only held by men who had sworn their allegiance to their precious PSA stewardesses. It's impossible to know how many men possessed these cards, but it was in the thousands, if not more.

Upon this card were these words:

This card identifies you as a member of the Precious Stewardess Association.

Club Rules
1. Must wear your PSA smile at all times.
2. Must fly PSA whenever you are flying within California.
3. Must be kind, considerate, helpful, and understanding of others (especially your charming PSA stewardess).
4. Must bring a token of your precious personality. i.e. candies, flowers or, for early morning, sweet rolls or donuts are happily and daintily devoured.

Remember, PSA stands for Precious Stewardess Association. If you are faithful in fol-

lowing these rules, you will be a life-long member of the Precious Stewardess Association. We hope to see you again on our flights.

This card wasn't handed out to just anyone – the person had to earn it. The first step to becoming a Precious Passenger was actually showing up with donuts or flowers for the girls, then requesting to be admitted to the club. The swearing-in ceremony took place in the front of the cabin where the eager man raised his right hand and swore to the above rules. The rest of the passengers roared with laughter. Many of them had taken the same oath.

On early morning flights, we always could count on a Precious Passenger to bring us donuts. On the afternoon flights, we received candy bars and the occasional bouquet of flowers. Any guy who brought roses was truly hoping to meet that special stew. Only heaven knows why we loved the donuts since we were all under such strict weight requirements!

As with so many things, this is unthinkable in the modern day. It's hard to even comprehend that it happened! But it did. And with the passage of time, our beloved Precious Stewardess Association faded into the sunset.

PART TWO

To see the Precious Stewardess Association card and

to get the full experience visit

https://www.tijuanatothecross.com/book/photo-experience/

and check out photos and new content now!

THREE BY THIRTY

From my tweens into adulthood, I was a very self-absorbed person. For teen-agers, this is somewhat normal. I'm embarrassed to say that my self-absorption continued well into adulthood. If I wasn't happy in a situation, I just left. I never saw the purpose of staying in something I didn't like. Why would I? No one told me any differently. Life was all about me and what made me happy, whatever that was.

By age thirty, I had been married and divorced three times. My one stability was flying with PSA. It became my life and refuge. I guess I took the old phrase "marry me and fly free" to a whole new level.

Out of respect for these men, I will refer to them as Strong and Sexy (SS, the man I was dating at the beginning of my flying career), Drill Sergeant (DS), and TWA Tom. They committed to these marriages, and I just walked out of the first two.

The third is a different story, but to get there, I must start with SS.

STRONG AND SEXY

In high school, a handsome guy two years older than me always walked by my house on his way home. I thought he was super dreamy. Jeans were just coming into style and, boy, did he look great in them. I remember exactly how he walked – slow, methodical, and with just the right amount of sway. He was working as an apprentice for an electrician, and I looked up to him. I cared mostly that he was an incredible hunk. His sweet, honest disposition came in a distant second.

During our first summer together, we spent a ton of time at the beach and in Tijuana, drinking. SS was a scuba diver and won my dad over by frequently bringing fresh lobster and abalone to eat. Abalone is a fantastic meat that is housed inside an ugly outer shell. However, the inside of the shell is beautiful and iridescent, like mother of pearl. The shell insides were often made into earrings. Sadly, over the years, abalone became overfished off the cold Pacific coastline and a moratorium was put on them. Few restaurants serve it today. Recently, a San Francisco restaurant had abalone on the menu for $47.00. Dad didn't like that SS always wore jeans, but he sure appreciated the abundance of abalone!

I will always remember the day SS and I started talking about getting married. It was July 20, 1969. Later that night, everyone in America and around the world watched as Neil Armstrong, Mission Commander of Apollo 11, first stepped foot on the surface of the moon. Pilot Buzz Aldrin joined him about twenty minutes later.

SS and I had just come back from the beach and taken a shower. He smelled like Coppertone or Sea and Ski. The sun was pouring into my bedroom, and we had the TV on. They were discussing the upcoming attempt to walk on the moon.

I don't remember our exact conversation, but we settled on the idea of eloping to Lake Tahoe. I would have agreed to anything he wanted or didn't want, but what guy really wants a wedding? Most girls dream of their weddings from childhood, but I didn't. I guess I felt like the idea of me walking down the aisle would be a mockery. Everyone would stare at me, knowing SS was far from the first. I felt used, not worthy. I didn't have many girlfriends who would want to be my bridesmaids. I didn't have much use for women. I always gravitated to the men at gatherings and parties; they were far more interesting.

Even if God had whispered in my ear that very moment that I was loved and special, I wouldn't have heard Him . My heart was closed to his love, a love I didn't know existed. SS and I never had a deep spiritual conversation. Not once.

Our parents agreed to our elopement, and SS and I left in October of 1969.

We flew into Lake Tahoe and drove to Carson City, Nevada, where a justice of the peace married us. We returned to Tahoe for a few days' worth of a honeymoon. We were young and in love and just wanted to play and travel. While dating, we agreed that we didn't want to have children. I was barely twenty years old.

SS was an electrician, and many of our couple friends were, too. Water skiing was our thing. We had special permits for a ski slalom area behind Sea World on Mission Bay. To keep the wake activity to a minimum, only two ski boats were allowed into the area at a time. The water was always smooth. When it was my turn, I popped out of the water on a single ski, stretched out, cut hard around each slalom buoy, and sprayed up a huge rooster tail of water. On longer weekends, we headed to the Colorado River with our ski boats.

We used my airline passes to travel to Tahiti, a very exotic trip for two young lovers. The next year, we went to Italy. It started to look like a fun international trip would take place on a yearly basis. We bought a cute, adorable, two-bedroom one-bath home off 70th and University in La Mesa, slightly east of San Diego State. I could make it to the airport in twenty minutes.

At the beginning, SS was my knight in shining armor, except he drove a motorcycle and wore tight jeans. However, it didn't take me long to outgrow my feelings for this handsome, kind, good, sexy, decent man who loved me. I didn't think he was sophisticated enough. After all, I was flying with airline people. I wanted out.

Honestly, I began to bait him. If he didn't like onions in something, I added in extra and then said he wasn't worldly enough. I started saying how I wanted children, and he reminded me that we agreed we didn't want any. He was ready to get a vasectomy. I wasn't happy.

During this time period, my parents sold the Square Bottle and moved to Payson, Arizona, ninety miles northeast of Phoenix. I told my parents I wasn't happy in my marriage. They stressed that I should give it more time to work out, but they said that whatever I wanted to do was fine with them. If I was unhappy, they understood. Wow! They didn't discuss marriage as something to be dedicated to or to fight for. They didn't suggest counseling or any other option before making a final terrible decision that would tear lives apart. My happiness was at the top of their list.

I took more flights to get away from home and blamed it on scheduling. I said we were short on stewardesses to cover flights. It was an easy way to lie. I added myself to the holiday schedule, allowing other girls who had children the time off. My real motivation was avoiding all of my family issues. I never spent an adult Christmas with my mom and dad. With SS, I kept poking the bear, creating issues instead of trying to heal wounds. After all, I wasn't happy.

I realized that if I was going to depart from this marriage, I needed to start socking away more money. I asked the scheduler for even more flights. At the time, we were paid by the mile.

Two particular flight segments stood out – the 1867 and the 1495. The numbers represented the miles flown. The 1867 consisted of twelve take-offs and landings, and the 1495 had sixteen! Both routes were full of short flights up and down the scenic California coastline from San Diego to San Francisco. I earned $9,000 in 1972.

Around this time, we got new uniforms. Out with our orange ruffled pettipants and in with hot pants and go-go boots! Our dresses barely covered our fannies. They were red with pink swooshes down the middle and matching red calf-high boots or light orange with a wide pink panel and orange boots. We wore matching short shorts underneath our dresses, and our jackets had large S-shaped zippers from hem to neck and fell just above our dress. The jackets didn't add much warmth. These uniforms were such a hit with the California male travelers that several commercials were made. For a culture lesson and to see our uniforms, go to YouTube and look up "Ronnie Schnell and PSA Stewardess 1972 Commercial." Please – go right now! It was also around this time that we started sneaking flats into our carry-on bags, changing into them for serving.

Our uniforms weren't the only things that changed in the early '70s. Much like the crumbling of my marriage, the feeling of security in the skies also began to crumble.

My flying career began before security checks. People were able to walk out on the tarmac. Boyfriends, girlfriends, spouses, and friends all greeted passengers as they got off the airplane.

On January 7, 1972, a couple boarded a PSA airplane. They were carrying what appeared to be a sleeping baby in a carrier, covered by a blanket. No one questioned them. Why would they?

After take-off, the man went into the restroom with the baby carrier and came out with a now-assembled shotgun. The plane was hijacked to Cuba. Fortunately, no one was hurt. I personally knew the entire San Diego-based crew who was working that flight. Their stories were terrifying!

Later that year, on July 5, another PSA flight was hijacked with demands to fly to the Soviet Union. The plane was stormed when it landed in San Francisco, resulting in the deaths of the two hijackers and a passenger. The actor who played

Hop Sing on *Bonanza* was also on this flight. He was shot, but he survived. This was the first hijacking in the United States where people were wounded and killed.

Over the next few years, many more hijackings occurred, and a preliminary type of security began. Still, airline crews were allowed to pass through by flashing their badges. The standard searches of today didn't come until years later.

Security wasn't the only major change to come to the flying public. The other big shift was the introduction of women passengers – not just mothers who were part of the weekend family crowds, but working women.

These women were the strong, determined, business-suit-and-briefcase type competing in a man's world. The Women's Liberation movement had begun! Songs like "I'm a Woman, W-O-M-A-N" and "These Boots Are Made for Walking" were constantly on the radio. Gloria Steinem and Bella Abzug marched for women to have equal opportunities, both to work and raise a family, to have it all and succeed all the way to the top. They were going to free all women from the drudgery of everyday life. Unfortunately, I don't think a stewardess was what they had in mind, especially one in hot pants and orange go-go boots.

I, too, was a working woman, supporting myself and making my own decisions. I wasn't sure why these women treated us the way they did.

On one morning flight, I was standing at the front door greeting passengers. Three women dressed in business suits came up the stairs and did not acknowledge my hello. They glared straight past me. Later, it came time to serve their row.

"Would you care for coffee or juice?" I asked politely.

I didn't get a response.

Perhaps they didn't hear me.

"Would you care for anything to drink?"

Again, they snubbed me.

I moved the cart about a foot down the aisle so I had room to kneel down beside their row.

"In case of an emergency or crash landing, *I* am the one who will get your asses off of this plane," I nicely said in a low voice.

I stood up and continued serving.

My comment must have resonated with them. For the remainder of the flight, they were very nice and even offered up a good-bye and thank you as they left. Maybe they realized I was a working woman, too.

By the middle of 1972, I decided to divorce SS and planned my strategy. I figured there was no need to discuss it with him; he might want to talk about it or go to counseling or something. Why do that when I'd already made up my mind? I never once considered him, his family, or our vows. I certainly did not consider God, and my parents had already given me the green light because I wasn't happy.

I came home from a trip one night, and he was already in bed but not asleep. I walked into the bedroom and he raised his arms toward me, indicating he wanted me to snuggle in for a hug. With little emotion, I flatly said I wanted a divorce. He sat in stunned silence. I announced that I would be sleeping in the other room from now on.

From that point until the divorce was final, I honestly don't remember much. I was emotionally checked out and already planning what to do with my newly found single life.

When I look back, my heart breaks at how cold and callous I was to this dear man. Oh, how I wish I could face him and apologize! Years later, I did write to him, confessing my sorrow and asking for his forgiveness. I still don't know if he received the letter or not.

DRILL SERGEANT

All throughout high school, I broke up with one boyfriend and immediately had to have another. With a divorce, I'd heard it was wise to take time to heal, recapture some confidence, and put the shattered pieces back together. However, following my own divorce, my insecurities and lack of self-worth kicked in, and I wanted a new boyfriend almost immediately. I dated a few men, but none were worth hanging on to.

Then, during one September afternoon flight, a Precious Passenger boarded our plane with a bunch of red roses for the stewardesses.

I lived in San Diego and he lived in Marina Del Rey with two cats. He did something with technology and computers in hospitals. In 1974, any job with computers put a person on the cutting edge of the future. He traveled frequently and flew PSA often. The roses did it and we started seeing each other whenever his and my schedule allowed.

Right off the bat, I noticed this guy was super high energy. He didn't know how to move at a slow pace and dove into everything like a drill sergeant. Actually, he had been a drill sergeant out of the Marine Corps Recruit Depot in Parris Island, South Carolina. He was ten years older than I was, and strong – exactly like a stereotypical Marine. Since he was older, he had a nice car and we went to nice restaurants. We played golf – a *lot* of golf – and that was just the beginning of our intense activities. Of course, he said he didn't want children to interfere with all the fun, so I said I didn't want children either. I certainly didn't want to do or say anything that would put up roadblocks in this rapidly blossoming relationship.

Drill Sergeant wanted to teach me to snow ski. I wanted to be his dream come true, ready and willing for all of his adventures. We headed to Mammoth Mountain for my first ski lesson, and, in true Marine fashion, DS led me straight to the top of a black diamond run. It was a *long* way to the bottom and my own bottom froze from being on it most of the way down. But I matched his Marine intensity and proudly stood at the end of the run, ready to go back up. Oorah!

We played golf the same way. We started early in the morning so we could finish eighteen holes by lunchtime and play another eighteen after. Soon, we were talking marriage. Because he loved golf so much, we decided to elope to Hawaii where we could play thirty-six holes every day!

Like before, my parents were fine with us eloping – whatever made me happy. And like before, we had no spiritual conversation about the vows we would be making. We contacted The Fern Grotto on the island of Kauai and pre-arranged for a justice of the peace to meet us there. Off we went, just the two of us – no family or witnesses to celebrate, just us and thirty-six holes of golf. That was the way we wanted it.

DS was a good man. He was faithful, loyal, strong, loved me, and loved my mom and dad. I never met his mom and his dad had passed away, so my parents became his family.

We returned from Hawaii and settled into life, skiing every weekend at Mammoth Mountain. During the spring and summer months, DS introduced me to white water river running. We headed north to the Tuolumne and Stanislaus rivers. These rivers hit their flood stage from the snow melt coming off the Sierras. I loved this part of Northern California, full of stories about the Gold Rush. Even Highway 49 was named after the miners of that era.

I loved being on the river. We slept outside, zipping our sleeping bags together so we could snuggle and fall asleep under the stars. It was a refreshing respite from the airplane and its dirty air. I actually became good at reading a river, watching its flow and seeing where the underwater boulders were. I was good at predicting where the current would go as I worked my nine-foot oars in the heavy water.

After a while, we grew weary of driving over 700 miles every weekend and made the decision to move to the Bay Area. I stayed based out of San Diego where I had my choice of trips. If I'd changed to San Francisco, I would've been at the bottom of the seniority list, maybe even on reserve. We eventually built a four-bedroom home in Pleasanton in the East Bay Area, south of Walnut Creek. As for golf, we always managed to fit it in when we had an empty four-to-five hour slot.

THE GRAND CANYON

For two years, DS and I ran rivers at flood stage to prepare for the granddaddy of them all – the Colorado River. Winding 225 miles through the Grand Canyon, rafting it is the ultimate rugged trip. It would last for two weeks.

We had formed a merry band with other raftsmen on the Stanislaus, meeting on the weekends and rafting rivers that only the experienced would attempt. DS and I didn't fit the mold of the average river rat. We had jobs, we weren't skinny, and we didn't have long, stringy, dreadlock-type hair. Regardless, we formed a tight-knit supportive crew with our friends.

We rode two to a raft. Our raft was a thirteen-foot Avon, sturdy and super-well made. Our pontoons kept us only fifteen inches off the water. The rest of our company had similar professional equipment.

To run the Canyon, an application was required. The Bureau of Land Management (BLM) turned down our first application in 1975, saying we didn't have enough heavy water experience. We needed to run the Kings Canyon River at flood stage. Roaring down out of the Sierras, Kings Canyon had approximately the same river volume that the Colorado did on a normal day. After we completed that, we had to document the type of equipment we used, the first aid supplies we had, and all the other rivers we had run. One of the guys in our group was an EMT, so he verified that he could splint a broken bone, do stitches, and administer prescription-level meds for pain. We submitted our application again and were approved.

We were given a push-off date of August 1976. We were officially privateers, independent of the need for an organized rafting company. Other folks seeking this adventure had to hire a company and be taken down the river in much larger rafts, but not us. All in all, we had six rafts and one kayak. Besides DS and me, our crew consisted of eleven guys and a girl from the BLM who was assigned to our trip.

We prepared for months. Finally, we arrived in Flagstaff on a hot August night. Early the next morning, a transport took us and our equipment to the starting point called Lee's Ferry, just south of Lake Powell in Marble Canyon. The canyon walls were wide here; further down the river, the walls eerily tightened in on us. There were also places downriver where the walls opened up wide again and the water slowed, revealing beaches on either side.

We left our keys with the transport company. They drove our cars toward Lake Mead outside of Las Vegas. Our pullout was 225 miles downriver. In two weeks, our cars would be waiting for us at the Indian trading post at Peach Springs, just off the river at Diamond Creek.

We spent the night on the riverbank at Lee's Ferry. In the morning, we got an early start. Our equipment had to be inspected and approved by our female agent from the BLM. After she had finished, we pushed off into the muddy, ice-cold Colorado River. The air temperature hovered around 105 degrees, but the water was so cold that we threw our daily ration of beer overboard in a heavy mesh sack. If rocks or rapids were ahead, we hoisted it back on board – anything to save the beer! In the afternoons, we enjoyed an icy cold one.

The adventure began marvelously. Each day before shoving off, we examined all of our ropes and tie-downs to make sure the rowing platform was secure. An extra set of ten-foot oars was strapped to the side of the raft, and all personal items – like my camera, glasses, and Tuaca, an Italian Liqueur – were inside waterproof bags or Army ammunition boxes. Nothing could be loose. There was always a possibility of flipping, and loose items could wrap around us, drag us down river, or trap us under the water. We were highly cautious.

When a rapid was coming up, we pulled ashore, tied up our rafts, and hiked downriver to look at it. We analyzed which way the river current was flowing and what obstacles we needed to row away from, like huge rocks, drop-offs, or jagged ledges. I soon found out that the bigger the rapid, the stronger the pee smell on shore was. I guess every guy took a leak after checking out the river, especially before the scariest ones.

The international rating of rapid difficulty is I to VI, but the Colorado River uses a 1-10 scale instead. The most famous class 10s we had ahead were Crystal Rapid and Lava Falls, but I figured I had days to prepare for these big boys. Both of these monsters were past Phantom Ranch, a beautiful stay-over camp that folks hiked down to from the rim. We were going to pass Phantom Ranch at the six-day point of our trip. Our first major rapid was House Rock, a mere class 4.

As we approached, we tied up our rafts and hiked downriver to analyze House Rock. The rapid was appropriately named – the rock was as big as a house, mostly underwater, with rushing water pouring over it into a boiling, angry, white frothy mess. The strongest current flowed straight toward it, so we planned our maneuvers to row backwards and catch another current before that one caught us. By doing this, we would completely avoid House Rock. We'd all done this type of maneuver a hundred times – easy peasy. No wonder it was only labeled a class 4.

DS and I won the toss to go first. Our fellow river rats hiked down to film us going through our first official big rapid. We checked everything and pushed off. DS was prepared to start back-rowing as soon as we got around the reeds. We took our time and drifted a bit as we floated out into the river.

It didn't take long to realize this river was bigger, stronger, and more powerful than anything we had been on before. No amount of muscle could have pulled us out of the direction we were headed – straight toward House Rock. We were swept up on top of the rock and spun sideways. We teetered on the edge for a moment, and then it dumped us upside down into the boiling mash below. All I remember was being sucked under, the raft on top of me, the water pulling me in all directions like I had never felt before. I was sure I was going to die; then, all of a sudden, I popped up out of the water like a cork, desperately taking great gulps of air.

DS popped up gasping for oxygen as well. Our raft was still upside down; the churning of the water kept sucking it back against the rock. Finally, it too was let loose by this monster. A joint effort from the other rafters along the riverbank saved our raft. Quite a way downriver, we were able to get ourselves ashore. Not one thing was lost or torn loose from our now upright raft. Exhausted, we made camp.

DS was concerned about me. When he noticed I was super quiet, he was truly sweet. I was frightened to death. I was furious he would bring me on such a trip, even though I had been excited for the adventure. This rapid had been just a 4 for heaven's sake! What the hell were we going to do with the 8s, 9s, and 10s? There was nothing but bigger rapids ahead of us. I couldn't sleep that night out of fear of what was coming. I shivered as I stared out into the blackness. We were a mile deep from the canyon rim. Up above, the stars looked so peaceful. I drank my Tuaca and thought about the beast of a river before me.

The rest of the group learned from our mistake of miscalculating the drift. For the remainder of the trip, we were the only ones who flipped.

The next thirteen days were full of the most majestic scenery I'd ever experienced. The river left little time for romance or sex, but DS looked awesome, strong, and tanned in his massive life jacket with sun-bleached chest hair glistening beneath. We shared a ton of laughter, great food, cold beer, nightly Tuaca, and, of course, the rapids. Over the 225 miles, we crossed eighty-five of them.

God's artistry was on display in this stunningly beautiful, rugged place. Words cannot adequately express how happy and simultaneously afraid I was on this river. DS understood my fear. When it came to the really big rapids, I became the official photographer and hiked my way around. We had to cover fifteen miles each day so we could be off the river in two weeks and, sadly, return to our normal lives.

It's funny what a person craves when away from civilization for two weeks. When we walked into the Peach Springs Indian trading post to retrieve our car keys, I grabbed a quart of ice-cold milk and chugged it. Absolute bliss!

JESUS MOVEMENT

In Southern California in the early '70s, a major movement was happening that affected me vastly more than I realized. It was called the Jesus movement.

During this time, my fellow flight crew members started reading Bibles and inviting me to Bible studies. Around San Diego Bay, large groups were gathering. I thought they were having parties, but I discovered it was people getting baptized. What in the world was going on?

I was flying in and out of Hollywood Burbank a ton, much more so than usual. Maybe that was God's plan. Who knows? Every time we had a turnover in Burbank, the ground crew came on board to help us clean up, cross seat belts, grab coffee, and just talk. I became especially good friends with a tall blond ground agent I called Curly and two baggage handlers who reminded me of Sammy Davis Jr. and Danny DeVito. These men were part of this Jesus movement, and I knew they were praying for me.

Back home, DS started to drive me nuts with his intensity. He insisted on accomplishing things completely by ourselves. We installed a sound system for our new house, complete with speakers mounted high in the corner of every room controlled by secret panels. Before the sheetrock went up, we laid all of the hidden wiring ourselves and created a special closet for the equipment. We designed and executed our own landscaping, too. We excavated, installed the sprinkler system, poured tons of rocks to make a sixty-foot winding dry creek to cover a drainage ditch (a really cool idea, actually), dug post holes for the eight-foot fence, mixed cement, planted twenty-five-gallon trees and tons of bushes, built a deck and gazebo, and laid the sod. We also still played golf, ran rivers, and whizzed down mountains in between my commutes to San Diego. Somewhere in our crazy life, we still found time to be in bed together at the same time. I was exhausted and getting burnt out.

I fantasized that people in San Diego were having fun and living relaxed lives, making love in the moonlight on the beach. My friends kept asking me to join them for a Wednesday night Bible study, but I was busy flirting with a co-pilot, a lot.

The co-pilot was married and had small children. We had a layover together and, as you can imagine, one thing led to another and we ended up in his room. Then we had another layover together, and another. My girlfriends wanted to know if I could bid for Thursday trips and fly in the night before so I could go to a Wednesday night Bible study with them.

Hmmm, Bible study or have an affair? Bible study or have an affair?

I honestly didn't care which one. I decided to tell DS I was going to San Diego for the Bible study.

I got in touch with SS and made arrangements to stay with him. I can't believe he even spoke to me after the way I walked out on him! But he was my first husband, so it was fine, right? I honestly think DS wasn't a bit concerned about me going down a night early; he trusted me. I lied and said I was staying with a girlfriend. He had no reason to doubt me. I fell into the habit of going down early whenever I could.

My soul was so dark. I was lying to my second husband about going to a Bible study while both sleeping with my first and having an affair with a married co-pilot. My friends Curly, Sammy, and Danny continued to pray for me. I was a mess.

Even so, God was at work in me. I have no idea why, but on my commutes, I started listening to an old-time preacher by the name of J. Vernon McGee. In his heavy southern accent, McGee preached a program called "Thru the Bible" on his radio show where he walked through the entire Bible from Genesis to Revelation. I was being exposed to things I had never heard. Week after week, I was hearing God's word.

I didn't tell my friends I was in San Diego on Wednesday nights; that way, I had no accountability. Deep down I guess even I was too embarrassed to tell anyone I was sleeping with my ex. Another bizarre reason I didn't tell them was that I wanted to go on my own and check out a popular Wednesday night church service I had heard about.

The service was at the old North Park Theatre. I pulled up to the full parking lot and heard loud drum and guitar music pouring out the open windows. Several cars had surfboards tied down on the roof racks, and two guys walked in with sand still on their feet, wearing just T-shirts thrown over their bathing suits. Everyone was comfortably casual, except for a few in business clothes who appeared to be coming straight from work.

It was 6:00 p.m. and the place was nearly full. I walked in with no clue what to expect. People were singing along to the music, some standing, some raising their hands, some sitting, some kneeling. Clearly, people did whatever they wanted.

Pastor Mike MacIntosh came on stage and began the service. He said a couple of funny things but then went directly to the Bible. Everyone had their own Bible and was reading from it. Weird.

I began to go to this church every Wednesday, but I was still staying at SS's apartment, flying and sleeping with my married co-pilot, and lying to my husband.

As this happened week after week, I began to be disgusted with myself. What was I doing, and why? DS was a great guy; we just needed to talk through some things, but communication was not his strong suit. Beyond that, I felt like there was a gigantic hole in my gut that wasn't satisfied. Why? There had to be more to life.

Pastor Mike preached about Jesus and said he died for me. If I believed in Him, asked for forgiveness, and sought Him with my whole heart, I could be in heaven for all eternity and never have to fear death or be alone again. But I didn't really understand – why did I need forgiveness? I didn't have any sins. I thought sins were big things like murder, bank robberies, or blowing things up.

Back home, I started to tell DS about this church and how awesome it was. However, I immediately told him what he needed to do while making few changes in my own life. I did throw out all my books on witchcraft, demons, and astrology. I was being told that all I needed was God's word, and it sounded like he ruled over all this other stuff – something about Him being King of kings and Lord of lords. That's what all the worship songs said, anyway.

One Wednesday night in the summer of 1977, Pastor Mike asked if anyone wanted to ask for forgiveness of their sins and ask Jesus into their life. I walked forward. I said a quick prayer, asking Jesus to forgive me and be in my life. This may have been driven by a popular book about the end times called *The Late Great Planet Earth* by Hal Lindsey. This book scared me to death; if I weren't a Christian by the time of the rapture – whatever that was – then I would be left behind to face the worst of end-time horrors.

I can barely believe it, but after that church service I still went back to SS's apartment. Sex with an ex-husband can be exciting, but someone will eventually get hurt. I started to feel that the hurt party once again might be SS, and I truly didn't want to hurt him again. That night, I realized we had to call it quits and once again go our separate ways. It was not as painful for him as the first time. He knew we had just been taking advantage of each other, for however long it lasted. I also finally broke it off with the co-pilot. I was thinking about his wife and children and how devastating it would be if they found out. Finally, I thought about someone other than myself.

I tried to read my Bible, be good, and talk to DS about how I'd changed. However, like a coal that has rolled away from a fire, my flame burned out. Without other Christians around me in Northern California, my passion slowly began to grow dim and cold. I had no one to keep me accountable, so nothing in my life really changed. It didn't take long for me to think this wasn't very fun, so I went back to my old ways.

My attention turned toward DS and how much he really was bugging me. I fell into the same habits I'd had with SS; I provoked DS into conversations I knew would irritate him. He would clam up, and then I'd accuse him of not talking to me. As I did with SS, I said I wanted to have children. DS reminded me that we'd agreed we didn't want children. He truly didn't, and he said that was what attracted him to me. San Diego was becoming more attractive to me all the time.

I talked to Mom and Dad. Once again, they said they'd stand behind whatever made me happy, even though they genuinely loved DS. I wonder what they really thought. Did they feel like I was going off a cliff yet still didn't offer any guidance? Maybe they tried, but I didn't want to hear it. A twenty-seven-year-old woman should not approach her second divorce without any questions. But I was going to do what I wanted to do, no matter what.

In November of 1977, I served DS with divorce papers. He was shocked, bewildered, and confused. I'll never forget the pained look on his face. He retreated to our bedroom, locking me out. He stayed in there for two days.

What have I done? I thought. His reaction was so intense.

However, it didn't take me long to realize that I was free and could move back to San Diego. The remorse I had over hurting DS quickly dissipated. I packed up my personal items and drove south. In hindsight, my heart aches so much for what I did. Why did I just walk out? Why did I rip hearts apart?

To this day, I have no idea how to find DS. If I could, I would ask for forgiveness. Not only did I tear apart our marriage, but I did this after I told him that I'd asked Jesus into my heart. He must have thought I was such a hypocrite! This is one of my deepest regrets. I pray he has found Christ himself, and that our marriage never crosses his mind.

Back in San Diego, I settled into a new townhome in Point Loma and quickly adjusted back to a more relaxed lifestyle. A handsome, single, ex-Navy co-pilot I knew owned a fancy ski boat and just happened to offer himself and his boat to four of us flight attendants on our Tuesday mornings off. Water skiing on Mission Bay on a weekday in the early morning hours was incredible. There were no crowds, and the water was as smooth as a glassy mirror. Afterward, we enjoyed brunch by the ocean and prepared for a 2:30 p.m. check-in for work. On Wednesday evenings, we enjoyed beer can races. We filled up about 500 water balloons and headed out into San Diego Harbor. Sailboats launched out to the end of Point Loma, turned around, and headed back into the bay. While this was happening, all the boats bombed each other with water balloons, trying to soak as many people as possible while staying sober enough not to fall overboard.

And so went the summer of '78.

SEPTEMBER 25

After I moved back to San Diego, two poignant events really made me start to think about eternity. Both things happened on September 25 – one in 1978 and one in 1979.

Flying is the safest mode of transportation. It is far safer than a car. Every year, more than five million car accidents occur compared to just twenty flying accidents. The chances of a plane crash are one in every 1.2 million flights. The chances of dying in a car accident are one in 5,000. In my twenty-eight years of flying, I never encountered anything more than yucky turbulence and rough landings.

However, though the chances are small, accidents do still happen.

In 1978, San Diego was the third busiest airport in the world with a single runway and a steep approach. Still today, planes fly in close to the downtown skyscrapers off to the captain's left side. Cars at the intersection of Laurel and Pacific Highway can look up and see planes landing about 300 feet overhead.

September 25, 1978 was a beautiful, clear Monday morning. I was off that day. Thirty of my fellow crew members and friends were deadheading home on Flight 182 from Los Angeles. (Deadheading is when a person rides a plane in uniform but as a passenger for the purpose of getting back home or picking up another flight route.) The total number of people on board was 135.

A small private Cessna was also flying in the vicinity with two people onboard. Both planes acknowledged to the tower that they had sight of each other. Then, they didn't.

It took ten seconds for the PSA plane to plunge nose first into a quiet North Park neighborhood going 300 mph, exploding into a million pieces. Everyone onboard both planes and seven people on the ground died.

One thousand one, one thousand two, one thousand three, one thousand four, one thousand five, one thousand six, one thousand seven, one thousand eight, one thousand nine, and then – one thousand ten.

In the blink of an eye, in that nanosecond, 144 souls stepped into eternity.

Where did they go? Heaven or hell?

Once the news hit, phone lines went crazy as loved ones tried to connect with each other. The city of San Diego was in shock. DS called me around noon to make sure I was alive. He said it was great to hear my voice, and that was the last time I ever talked to him.

For the next ten days, all I did was go to funerals, sometimes attending two or three a day. My friends and I became numb. For years, I had visions of my now deceased friends sitting next to each other, clinging together and screaming. Ten seconds is actually a long time to count down to death. Which side of eternity did they end up on?

The National Transportation Safety Board concluded that the accident was caused by an unauthorized course deviation by the Cessna pilots, poor separation techniques by the PSA pilots, controller errors, and a faulty collision warning system. It clearly highlighted several problems with the "see and avoid" principle, especially in high-speed aircraft environments.

Exactly one year later, on September 25, 1979, another major event happened. This one involved my dad.

As I referenced before, my dad was a man's man. He loved his cigarettes, bourbon, gin, and Westerns. He dreamed of being a cowboy. My cousin's husband was the Deputy Sheriff of Gila County in Arizona. He was also a part of the Payson Mounted Posse, a type of search and rescue team. This part of Arizona, the high desert wedged to the east between Flagstaff and Phoenix, is some of the wildest, most mountainous and rugged land there is. My cousin's husband paved the way for my dad to volunteer with the Mounted Posse, and his dream came true. He and several others served as ambassadors to help with public events.

Payson had its rodeo during August, a month or so before September 25. This is the oldest continuous rodeo in the world with an incredibly fun end-of-summer weekend celebration. My dad rode in the parade with the Payson Mounted Posse. I was so proud of him. He was smiling from ear to ear, living out his dream. I have a great picture of him on his horse in full uniform. With his full head of silver hair and his cowboy hat, he looked a bit like my teenage idol, Ben Cartwright, the dad on *Bonanza*.

During the entire weekend, he kept coughing. Mom and I insisted he go to the doctor the next week. Stubborn as he was, he never went.

About a month later, Dad was rushed to Good Samaritan Hospital in Phoenix on September 25. He stayed in the hospital for two weeks. Mom and I stayed at a resort called The Pointe where employees from all airlines hung out. On our first Saturday there, we met a polite, chatty, handsome man who worked for TWA, my uncle's airline. He was based out of Kansas City. We told him about my dad's hospital stay and he offered his well wishes.

The second Saturday, this same TWA man greeted us at the pool with a warm, "Hello again! How's your dad?" That Sunday evening, I kissed Dad good-bye.

"See you next week, probably up in Payson," I said as I left.

Dad died early the next morning on October 8, 1979.

My dad reminded me so much of the rugged Marlboro man from the '60s and '70s, and cigarettes are what ended up killing him. He was buried in his Posse uniform with his cowboy boots on and honored with a three-gun salute.

Unfortunately, I have no idea what he believed or whether I will ever see him again. I never heard him talk once about God, Jesus, heaven, or the Bible. I don't know if he ever prayed. The closest thing to him being spiritual that I ever experienced was when he made me go to church. He just thought it was a good idea, but he never offered to take me.

Believe it or not, the following September 25 brought yet another horrible incident. This one involved the TWA man I met at The Pointe Resort. We'll call him Tom.

TWA TOM

In the late '70s, security and privacy was not what it is today. TWA Tom, the man who I'd talked to at The Pointe Resort, learned what happened with my dad by calling the hotel front desk. He even got my address and phone number from them, making up some story about how he wanted to send flowers for the funeral.

Tom started calling me and even sent flowers to my home. Then, he came to San Diego for a visit. Goodness knows why, but Mom was thrilled.

"God took one man from us and gave us another!" she said.

Tom was a charmer, and he schmoozed us both.

Tom and I talked every day and saw each other most weekends. He had employee passes on TWA, so it was easy for him to fly out to be with me. On New Year's Eve, he whisked me back to Kansas City on a first-class flight to meet his folks and, along the way, proposed. Again, my mom was thrilled.

Tom's parents owned a huge farm in Kansas complete with massive machines called combines that helped with the harvest. His brothers owned large farms adjacent to the parents. They all seemed delighted to meet me and to see how happy Tom was. We met with his pastor for pre-marriage counseling. Surely, this was going to be a solid marriage.

We planned a March wedding. Tom had two kids from a previous marriage, and I even spoke with his ex-wife to assure her that I'd abide by whatever rules she had established when the kids were with us. She and I were going to work together and make this a solid arrangement for the kids. She wished me well and said good luck. I should have wondered what she meant by that.

Tom and I decided to put both of our houses on the market and keep whichever one didn't sell first. My San Diego condo sold within a few weeks, and the escrow money was wired to our joint checking account in Kansas City. We flew out to San Diego, packed up my stuff in a U-Haul, and drove through Payson to get my dad's beautiful old wood and glass gun cabinet, along with a few of his rifles. We kissed Mom good-bye and moved everything to his Kansas City three-bedroom townhome. I was so excited to be a stepmom!

From Kansas City, I had to commute to San Diego to pick up my flights. A rumor was circulating that PSA pilots were going to strike. Tom and I quickly decided to take the upper hand, and I put in for a six-month leave of absence, allowing us to settle into our marriage and spend our first Christmas with his children. I didn't have to be back to work until the first day of 1981.

After my last flight, Tom picked me up at the Kansas City airport in an expensive brand-new yellow Cadillac, decked out with all the extras. He grinned so big and said it was ours.

"Ours? What do you mean?" I said. "Where did you get the money?"

Tom snapped back.

"From the checking account."

This was the joint account where the escrow money from my condo sale had been deposited. I was dumbfounded. There had been no discussion, and we certainly did not need a new car. We had two perfectly nice cars.

"I don't know what you're so upset about," he said. "The money is ours to spend. What difference does it make?"

He surprised me again when he quit his TWA job and announced that we were moving to Houston. I started to question him, and his eyes turned black.

"I'm the provider around here. I'm going to do what is best and moving to Houston is it. End of story."

We rented a huge home way out on the northern outskirts of Houston, surrounded by towering Loblolly pine trees. The trees were so close together that it was impossible to see out – or in.

Tom was never home. I had no clue what he was doing. When I asked, I just got a look of extreme annoyance. Our sex life had become cold and aloof, just an ugly physical need fulfilled for him. I became paranoid. When his car drove up, I was terrified. He worked out and was strong at six feet tall.

One day, Tom came home, got one of my dad's shotguns, and grabbed me.

"Let's go," he said.

I had no choice.

We walked out into the piney woods. My heart was pounding.

I'm going to be shot dead out here in these woods.

He never spoke. He shot a few beer cans, tried to shoot some squirrels, shot a few tree trunks, and then we walked back. Once we were back in the house, his eyes turned as black as coal and his jaw formed a hard, chiseled line.

"I want you out of here. I hate you. Get your clothes and get out."

In shock and slightly relieved I was still alive, I ran to a smaller bedroom and locked myself in. I called my brother to come get me. Tom was truly Jekyll and Hyde. I was afraid of him – extremely afraid.

I didn't sleep that night. I moved the dresser in front of the door and sat there, listening for any noises outside in the hallway. When I heard his car leave the next morning, I finally relaxed enough to breathe. My brother arrived from Arizona that afternoon and we packed up my clothes and personal belongings. While Tom was still gone, we got out and headed for my mom's in Payson.

I left Texas on September 25, 1980, the anniversary of my friends' deaths and my dad's hospital stay. At this point, I was already dreading September 25, 1981.

Prior to Tom, I had a really cute townhome in Point Loma, a premier location in San Diego. Now, I had nowhere to live. Since I'd taken leave from my job, I couldn't return to flying until the first of the year, and I couldn't even draw unemployment. All the money that had been in our joint account was gone. I had nothing – no savings, no equity, and no job for four more months. What was I supposed to do?

My brother dropped me off at Mom's, and I settled in with nowhere else to go. As I told my mom what had happened, we both kept getting angrier. She was mad because someone had taken advantage of her baby. (She never thought about how her baby was the one who'd walked out on two other perfectly decent men). Mostly, I talked and she listened. Because of my dad's angry outbursts, Mom had learned to keep quiet and just let things play themselves out. She was wisely doing the same with me. As we talked, we came up with a plan, and I just happened to know of a friend who could execute it.

I came to know this friend from one of my flights early on in my career. Over the years, we developed an unusual relationship. If I had a layover in Los Angeles or Burbank, we met for dinner. Like my job with PSA, he was always there for me, through all my boyfriends and divorces. He was always available to talk and never judged me or asked about my motives or actions. I always came away with the feeling that he and his family – a large, strong extended family with lots of uncles from Armenia – were connected to the mafia. I figured if I ever needed something done, my friend had a friend who could do it.

I called him up and explained everything that Mom and I had discussed. If

Tom died before the divorce was final, I would get the life insurance. How could I be a suspect since Tom was in Texas and I was all the way in Arizona? This plan would get me back on my feet. I could get on with my life as it used to be. No one in San Diego had yet heard what Tom had done to me, so I could play the grieving widow to perfection. Obviously, this was well before *Dateline*.

I honestly was not prepared for what my friend said to me.

"No, I care about you too much," he said. "No matter what, it will always come back to you. They will track you down."

He didn't deny the possibility of taking care of Tom or say that the request was an uncommon one, but he cared too much about me to fulfill my wishes.

My mother and I never again discussed my foolish plan. I guess my friend was right to put a stop to my insane idea. Thank heavens he did; otherwise, I might be in prison writing this. I came to realize my mom had a silent type of wisdom. She knew how angry I was at Tom, how furious I was about losing everything. Just having her there as a mom to listen helped calm me down. I never knew how special she was until it was too late. I'm now a mom myself, and I wish I could sit down with her and just talk, laugh, and cry.

With my murder plot foiled, I realized I had to take responsibility for what would happen next. I contacted a few friends in San Diego and explained my financial predicament in light of my upcoming divorce – again. I asked them to put out feelers for any type of short-term job opening or housing opportunity until I was able to return to flying in January.

I got a call from an ex-roommate who had a politician friend who was temporarily moving to Washington, D.C., with his family. They owned an amazing home in Del Mar, a gorgeous beach community just north of San Diego. The house had an unobstructed view of the Pacific, and they didn't want to leave it unoccupied. They needed a house sitter.

This secluded, wooded hideaway up in the cliffs became my peaceful refuge for the next four months. I honestly can't say I used it as a time to draw closer to God or even to reflect on the lives I had ruined, including my own. I didn't try to find my way back to a church or Bible Study. Few people knew where I was, which left few people praying for me. If my baggage handler friends Danny and Sammy had known where I was, they certainly would have been! Instead, I settled into a void of nothingness. But even though people didn't know where I was, God knew.

During this hideaway time, I returned to Kansas City to sign papers for the divorce. I learned from Tom's sister, his ex-wife, and his mom that Tom had attempted suicide, which was part of the problem with his first marriage. I stopped by to speak to the pastor who married Tom and me and ask why he didn't mention any of this. He figured I knew. I called Tom's mom and asked why no one told me how unstable he was. They all figured he had been up front with me about his bipolar situation. They all had hoped this marriage would work out and settle him down.

His mom later contacted me. She felt horrible that I'd lost my place in San Diego. She asked how much equity her son had spent and then sent me a check for $19,000 along with a dozen roses. This allowed me to put a down payment on a two-story studio townhome with a garage about three miles from Pacific Beach and Mission Bay.

In some ways, I felt like what Tom did to me was payback for what I had done to SS and DS. I deserved it. I was one month shy of turning thirty-one with three divorces to my name.

As the new year began, my life slowly returned to what I considered normal, and I was back at work. One abnormal thing happened, though – I swore off men. Instead, I signed up for tennis lessons, bought paint and wallpaper, and set my sights on making my new place a home. I planned ski trips with girlfriends with no men allowed. For the first time ever, I didn't feel the need to have a man complete me. My girlfriends were strong women in their own right, and I began to mirror their energy and ambitions.

Taking advantage of my travel benefits, I planned a visit to the Amazon Jungle with my friend Karen, a fellow flight attendant. We thought it might be a fun place to meet adventurous men. I made sure to pack my "Marry Me and Fly Free" T-shirt. (Wait. Hadn't I sworn off men?)

We flew into Quito, Ecuador. The Quito airport is at an altitude of 9,200 feet and is surrounded by the huge Andes mountains. It's an especially dangerous airport for landings and take-offs. After spending a day in Quito, we boarded a small jet that roared down the runway, the belly of the plane practically skimming the mountains. It was the scariest take off I've ever experienced. Everyone on board let out a collective sigh when we cleared the peaks.

About thirty minutes later, we landed in the Amazon Basin at an old, abandoned airfield once operated by an oil company. The plane dropped Karen and me off and zoomed away to the next jungle airfield.

Our canoe and guide were waiting for us. For over an hour, we motored downstream on the Napo River, past a dense jungle so thick that it was impossible to see inside. We cruised by a small village on stilts. Everyone on the shore waved at us. We drifted around the bend and arrived at our floating hotel, The Orellana, tied up on the shore.

Our hotel home for the next six days was on a barge that looked like an old Mississippi paddle wheel. Also on board were four flight attendants from Western Airlines and a couple from San Diego. Our stay turned out to be quite the National Geographic adventure, full of fabulous unknown food (we didn't want to know what it was), crazy local cocktails called Pisco Sours, and jungle hikes with our gorgeous nature guide named Adonis. He actually did look like the Greek god – so much for my swearing off my interest in men!

Adonis had been raised at a missionary linguistic compound called Limoncocha. He took us there and we were greeted by children, some brown and some blond. They ran up to him, giggling and tugging on him for attention. While there, I attempted to use a blow gun, which was fun. However, our idea of guys being adventurous in the Amazon jungle proved to be false.

"Men don't come here looking for adventure," Adonis said, laughing. "They would rather look for women on the beaches of Hawaii."

One afternoon, we were on the top deck of our flotilla, the gathering place for all activities (mainly drinking). I had one too many Pisco Sours and was talking about diving into the river. Thank heavens Adonis changed my mind by telling me about the twenty-five-foot Anaconda that lived beneath our boat. Right then, he pointed out another bright green three-foot-long South American river snake slithering right where I would have jumped in, its tongue flicking and head reared as if ready to attack whatever splashed in front of him. It truly was a fabulous trip.

In another girls only trip, I took Mom to Egypt and Rome. Mom had such a hard time relaxing in Egypt. She was petrified that I would be kidnapped. My TWA uncle had told us for years about the slave trade out of the Middle East. Young girls on college break disappeared and no one ever heard from them again. Today, we call this sex trafficking. When I climbed up on a camel ready to trot out past the pyramids, my mom looked at me with a face so full of fear that I knew I couldn't go. She was petrified she'd never see me again. Before I climbed down off the camel, they took a picture of me. Mom and I spent the rest of the day arm in arm, touring the museums in Cairo.

We stayed just as close together in Luxor, crossing the Nile River to the Valley of the Kings and King Tut's tomb. We really had the best time. When we traveled back to Cairo for the flight to Rome, armed military guards with machine guns were on the tarmac as we boarded our flight. Once we were on board and the airplane door closed, Mom finally relaxed.

Rome was perfect – the eternal city. We visited the Vatican, the Trevi Fountain, and the Coliseum. I arranged upgrades to first class for us on TWA and we flew home. Mom was happy and content, and I was so darn pleased that I managed to take her on a trip such as this. The passes and experience of an airline employee were priceless! Still, in the back of my mind, I wondered how I was going to explain my three divorces to the next guy. Was I beginning to see that life wasn't all about me being happy?

Once I was back home, my roommate and I counted up how many times I had moved since I started flying ten years ago. As the addresses added up, she jokingly told me that I needed to create a business card as a "quickie" moving specialist, so I did. Before cell phones, every move came with a new phone number. I kept adding the latest one, thinking it looked cute.

Sandee Stephanson
Moving Specialist and Quickie Interior Design

~~714-488-5309~~ ~~714-488-2967~~

714-484-8789   ~~714-484-3231~~

We thought handing this card out would be fun, but it wasn't. I quickly realized that experiencing twenty-three moves by the age of thirty was not normal or healthy. It wasn't anything but sad. The only stabilizing factor in my life was my job with PSA.

I made a real effort to do fun things to take my mind off what a loser I was and how empty my life had become. On a balmy Las Vegas evening in early May of 1981, our crew arrived at our motel as the sun was setting. The motel had a courtyard, so we all had our doors open. This was way before the current Las Vegas with all of its glitz and extravagance. The strip was truly just that – a strip with bright lights in the middle of the desert along the main street. The Flamingo, Dunes, Tropicana, and Golden Nugget had been around for a while, and Caesar's Palace had just been renovated.

The crew walked to a coffee shop to grab a bite, and I chose to stay back in my room. I was feeling melancholy and sorry for myself. I turned on the TV and *The Waltons* came on. I sat there by myself, watching this wonderful old-fashioned family that exuded love and sappy support. Granny and the parents were always there to give sound advice, and if anyone got angry, they made amends by bedtime.

As I watched this fantasy world, I sat on the motel floor and sobbed, crying out to a God I barely knew.

"Will I ever be happy? Will I ever have a family?"

God knew where I was, and He was near. I just didn't know it.

September 25 was only four months away, and I was already dreading it.

To see the Precious Stewardess Association card and

to get the full experience visit

https://www.tijuanatothecross.com/book/photo-experience/

and check out photos and new content now!

PART THREE

PHIL – MY LIFE, MY WORLD

I will never forget Memorial Day weekend of 1981.

On Thursday evening, my crew was preparing to board passengers on a flight from San Diego to Phoenix. It was a balmy, pleasantly warm night, just after sunset when the sky turns deep blue and the stars begin their evening twinkle. Standing at the forward boarding door, I watched the passengers as they walked across the tarmac from the terminal. Three guys stood out in their business suits because almost everyone else was already wearing their long weekend gear. People were in a festive mood.

At that time, PSA was running a promotion that encouraged us to collect business cards on every flight. After receiving them, our art department stamped them with our logo, laminated them, and mailed them back as luggage tags, complete with our pink and red colors and PSA smile. This promotion allowed PSA to build its ever-growing customer database, and passengers loved the heavy-duty luggage tags. They became highly coveted amongst male travelers.

Once all the passengers had boarded the flight, I made my standard, somewhat silly announcement about collecting business cards that would magically return as luggage tags. I walked down the aisle, gathering the cards, and I came to the three suits I'd spotted earlier. All three handed me their cards. The company name was unfamiliar to me.

"What's this?" I asked.

Two of the men laughed and pointed to the guy on the aisle.

"That's why we hired him. He just moved to town from New Orleans."

The business cards represented a family-owned, boutique, bougie-before-its-time hotel chain. The company consisted of beautiful resorts located mostly in San Diego, Scottsdale, and Cabo San Lucas. The company wasn't well known and relied on word of mouth for promotion. That's where the new guy, Phil from New Orleans (which I learned was pronounced "N'awlins") came in. His job was to market these beautiful hotels.

Out of pure courtesy and my love for San Diego, I had an idea.

"We should get together for tacos and beer and I'll show you around town."

For the first time ever, I seriously had no ulterior plans or motives. I honestly thought it would be fun to show this guy the great city of San Diego. He was thinking about a whole lot more. In the early '80s, we stewardesses were still known to take our appearance very seriously. The TV Show *Family Feud* asked the contestants, "What is the most glamorous job for women?" Stewardess ranked number one.

I gave him my phone number.

The following Tuesday, I received a phone call.

"Hi, this is Phil Mogle," he said. "We met on the flight Thursday night. I just got back from Scottsdale and I'd like to know if you'd join me for some Mexican food."

I never pass on Mexican food and I already knew I was off Thursday night, but I told him I'd check my flight schedule. I wanted it to sound like I was really busy.

We had our first date during the first week of June in 1981. Three more dates quickly followed, all with Mexican food. Thank heavens the man loved Mexican as much as I did! Over those dates and in the years that followed, I learned all about the life and family of this handsome, athletic, 6'4" tall guy.

Phil's father and mother, Richard and Alma, both graduated from the University of Southern California. Richard was an entrepreneur even from his early days. He founded the Aviation Club at USC, where he met Alma. She was a model for his newly founded club and wore one-piece flight suits. Alma also had a brilliant business mind and was the first woman to graduate from the USC School of Business in 1928. Richard and Alma got married and moved to Chino, California.

Richard was actively involved in water development across Southern California. He drilled wells for farmers and was hired by the developers of Sun City to bring water to Yucca Mesa, located next to Joshua Tree National Park. The plan was to develop a retirement community, but the developers filed for bankruptcy before the project got off the ground. Instead of being paid in dollars, Richard was given over 100 acres of high desert property in Yucca Mesa. Around this time, he also started the Mogle Water Company.

Richard and Alma had two daughters one after the other, Virginia and Patricia. The entire family was crazy for the beach. They had many friends with properties in Corona del Mar, Balboa Island, Newport Beach, and Laguna Beach, and they dreamed of building their own beach cottage for the family to enjoy. The ended up buying land in a secluded area called Emerald Bay with hopes of building the beach house in the future.

The girls have amazing memories of visiting Emerald Bay. Alma packed great lunches and they spent long, lazy days walking around the rocks and collecting shells and sand dollars. They made shell necklaces, built sandcastles, and rode rafts on the waves. A few years later, Phil was born and joined in on the adventures. His older sisters doted on him, and they have many happy memories from the beach and of riding horses in the Chino Hills.

Sadly, Richard died of cancer when Phil was only eight years old. After Richard's death, Alma designed and built a modest three-bedroom beach cottage with an expansive all-glass view of the Pacific Ocean. With both sisters now away for college at USC, Phil and Alma moved down to Emerald Bay permanently.

Alma continued running the Mogle Water Company until it was sold to Southern California Water in 1962. She also gradually sold off the Yucca Mesa property in 1.5-acre parcels. Alma Mogle was the first woman in Southern California to subdivide property! She kept meticulous records on 3x5 index cards in a recipe box. Each buyer paid monthly installments of $25.00.

As busy as she was, it could have been easy for Alma to neglect her family, but it was just the opposite. She took on the roles of both mom and dad and was a tremendous influence in her children's lives – and, much later on, in mine.

Phil excelled in all sports, including basketball, baseball, and – his favorite – football. He was a handsome star athlete and all-around nice guy, but he still was beaten out for student body president of Laguna Beach High School by a girl nicknamed "Granny Annie." It was the late '60s, the height of the drug revolution, so Granny Annie's victory probably had something to do with her hanging out at the local Taco Bell where everything was for sale, including tacos. Phil wasn't interested in anything Granny Annie was buying or selling.

Phil had been raised from birth to be a USC Trojan. *Many* family members were already USC graduates, and Phil loved USC more than anything. However, he knew there would be costs associated with attending college, so he became an offensive tackle at Golden West, a local junior college. He then received an All-Western Conference full scholarship to play football at Colorado State University in Fort Collins, Colorado. Since he had already played at the junior college, his eligibility only went through his junior year. For his senior year, he followed the family legacy of his thirty-four aunts, uncles, and cousins and graduated from the University of Southern California in 1974.

After graduation, Phil's first job was in the sales department at The Beverly Hilton hotel. Soon after, he had the wonderful opportunity to work in the marketing department at the New Orleans Marriott. In 1978, he won the company-wide award as the youngest Marketing Man of the Year. He became known for his ability to give convention attendees the best tour of N'awlins, extending well into the wee hours of the night (or should I say morning). Phil created the New Orleans Crawling Tour, a drink fest that crawled from one pub to the next. It started out the back door of the Marriott and came with a certificate of completion – for those who made it. Phil became known as Mr. Party of the hotel convention industry. For a good time, find Phil Mogle. He was excellent at making business connections and entertaining clients!

Phil was a promoter for Marriott, so he fully embraced the New Orleans lifestyle. At Easter time, he became the famous seven-foot bunny rabbit. He donned his rabbit costume complete with white feet and pointy ears and walked the Quarter. He even appeared in costume on the local TV sports station, typing away in the background like any other reporter. He always said it was amazing what women would say – and do – to a seven-foot bunny rabbit!

He participated in Pete Fountain's Half Fast Walking Club. Every week, he helped host the Joe Gemelli Sports Show from the lobby of the Marriott. He brought the entire USC Marching Band into the Marriott ballroom for a convention, and they rocked the house! He was a fixture at the finer dining establishments, many of which had a separate back door for the locals. He received personal greetings from all the dank French Quarter pubs. If there was a special client in the hotel, Phil was responsible for making sure they always chose Marriott for return visits. Conventions were successful because of Phil Mogle.

All the fun, women, rich sauces, butter, liquors, over-indulgences, and late nights eventually took their toll. Phil blew up to 350 pounds, and he knew he'd had enough. New Orleans was going to kill him and his kidneys if he didn't get out. It had already killed a brief marriage.

The only option with Marriott at the time was a move to Washington, D.C. Phil always felt an obligation to take care of his mom, so he felt the move wouldn't be wise. Plus, he simply needed a break. His bloated appearance was far from his playing years at Colorado State, and he felt a desperate need to detox and lose weight. His sister connected him with someone in the car rental world and he began building his own business. He worked hard on everything – the business, his weight, and his workouts. But the hotel convention industry was in his blood. He missed it.

He started putting feelers out, which led to Memorial Day weekend in 1981. He had moved back to San Diego and was taking his first business trip with his new company on my plane.

After four straight dates of Mexican food, the deal was sealed. By mid-July, we were inseparable, either at his place or mine. My uniforms found a permanent place in his second bedroom closet. Our weekends consisted of sleeping in late on

Saturday and then taking in whatever game he had tickets for. When I first met Phil, he had season tickets for the USC Trojans, the Dodgers, the Rams, and the Chargers!

When there wasn't a game on a Sunday, we headed to the grassy area on Mission Bay for volleyball and Bloody Marys. We played with Phil's coworkers, including the two friends that I'd met on the plane. Sometimes a ski boat was added to the mix, and I was on the water as often as I could grab a turn.

September 25 was coming up quickly. Phil knew of my dread fueled by the previous three years that had been so horrible – the crash of Flight 182, my dad going into the hospital, and Tom kicking me out of the house. On September 25, 1981, I was scheduled to fly and was a nervous wreck.

All day long, my brain had all sorts of horrific scenarios churning around. I was beyond relieved when my day ended with a safe landing in San Diego. We taxied to the gate, and I opened the forward door. As the ground agent pushed the stairs up to the door, I looked down and saw Phil standing on the tarmac holding a bouquet of flowers. The curse of September 25 had been broken – and so beautifully done. Oh, how this man had completely stolen my heart!

In October, we attended our first USC football game together. We cruised up the coast for two hours and arrived at The LA Memorial Coliseum. We parked in the season ticket holder lot and made our way to the tailgate where Phil's mom, sister, and USC alumni friends were gathered. Phil loved to watch pre-game warm-ups, so we headed in early to find our season seats. His mom and sister joined us as both teams came onto the field.

The minutes, touchdowns, penalties, cheers, and moans ticked away, and USC was losing. The family's frustration was visibly and verbally apparent.

Who are these people? I wondered.

Their passion for football was beyond anything I had ever experienced. They knew every play, every call, and every player, and their emotions were deeply embedded in what was happening on the field. My first USC football game ended in a loss.

We left the Coliseum and drove to a restaurant in silence.

It's just a game, I kept thinking. Thank heavens I didn't say that out loud!

A few minutes later, Phil's mom and sister joined us at the restaurant along with a few more extremely sad Trojans. Anyone watching us from afar would have assumed we'd just left the funeral of one of our closest relatives!

Phil's hotel chain had the only convention space in San Diego, and many of his New Orleans clients booked their conventions in San Diego just so they could be back with Phil Mogle. His fame and expertise in the industry continued to grow. When he traveled, I often jumped on an airplane to go with him. Over the next two years, luxury became the norm for us – beautiful hotels; extra-large suites with bottles of wine; fabulous dinners in NYC, Miami, and Chicago; cruises; trips to the theatre; skiing in Aspen; and summer season tickets to Shakespeare in Balboa Park. However, despite all the extravagance, something was tugging at Phil's heart – and my heart, too.

Phil's mom had found a church with sound Bible teaching that she loved. When we visited her in Laguna Beach, she occasionally asked us to go with her. Every time, we found an excuse not to go. We also pretended she had no clue we were sleeping together, but I knew she knew.

The summer of 1977 when I walked forward to accept Christ seemed like a lifetime ago. No one mentored me or showed me how or what to read. My decision meant nothing to me, and I turned my back and walked away. But still, God had planted a seed.

On a beautiful, sunny Sunday in 1983, Phil and I joined his mom to visit her church, Calvary Chapel of Costa Mesa. The church I had briefly attended was mostly full of beach kids and young people. This church was way different. Hundreds of people of all kinds – young, old, teens, professionals, and families – came from parking lots jammed with cars. Most of them were carrying Bibles. Maybe some of the same teens who'd been at my previous church were now here with their children.

Inside, the place was packed. Television screens outside allowed folks in the overflow areas to participate. The praise and worship music started, and the room was filled with drums, guitars, and beautiful voices singing songs about hope, eternal life, no more tears, forgiveness, and joy everlasting. The pastor asked everyone to open their Bibles. They actually did, and read from them! Weren't these things just meant to be paper weights on coffee tables in the living room? Over the next year, we returned a few times. The tugging grew stronger. I even noticed Phil watching a pastor on TV now and then, and I sometimes listened to praise and worship music in my car.

Obviously, something about our relationship was different than my previous ones. We were heading into our third year of dating with no mention of marriage. We truly loved each other; I couldn't imagine my life without Phil. But I had my condo and he had his. I was growing tired of splitting my life between two places, not really calling either one home. The old saying "Why buy the cow when you get the milk for free?" started to hit home. Phil had it made. He had no reason to put a ring on my finger.

In August of 1983, I played a long shot and told Phil I was moving permanently to my house. I needed stability in my life even if it meant going back to being single. I wanted a place that I could turn into a home – not a bachelor pad.

Our separation didn't last long; he couldn't stand to be without me. We set a wedding date for February 19, 1984. Phil convinced me that the idea of a wedding ceremony was far worse to him than the idea of being married. Even for a seven-foot bunny rabbit, he didn't like being the center of attention.

We told everyone we were having a birthday party at his mom's house, and it just happened to turn into our wedding. It was a beautiful day overlooking the Pacific Ocean. His cousin was a judge and married us quickly in a civil ceremony. Once again, there was no mention of God.

When Christmas was approaching later that year, Phil's mom was planning to spend it in San Diego with us. We knew she'd want to attend church but had no clue where to take her.

I called a local Christian bookstore and asked if they had any idea of a place where people actually read the Bible and sang along to upbeat praise music. She chuckled and asked where we lived.

"Yes, I have a few in mind, but I highly recommend Skyline Wesleyan in Lemon Grove. John Maxwell is the pastor there."

The spiritual scene in the '70s and early '80s was strange; I'd seen members of the Hare Krishna faith trying to recruit people in airports – my airports. They were mostly young hippies drawn to a new version of counterculture spirituality. They gave up their jobs, their homes, alcohol, drugs, and extramarital sex. They lived in remote communes and wore flowy orange saffron-colored robes while chanting and banging their tambourines. They were bold and brash and everywhere.

We wanted to make sure this Skyline Wesleyan wasn't anything like that, so we went the week before Christmas to check it out.

LIVES FOREVER CHANGED

We walked through the doors of Skyline Wesleyan Church on the morning of December 16, 1984, and it truly felt like Jesus Christ was there waiting for us with open arms.

After years of seeds planted and prayers from others, the tugging on our hearts was too strong to deny. I remembered my sobbing on the hotel floor, wanting forgiveness for destroying so many lives. Phil had similar regrets of using women and needing forgiveness. Finally, our hearts were completely open to the saving power of Jesus Christ.

Everything about the sermon that day plucked at our heartstrings. We realized that trusting in Jesus was the only solution for the pain we had both caused and felt. As we walked forward, we both had tears streaming down our faces. Later, Phil jokingly said the Holy Hounds of Heaven had been after us for a long time, nipping at our heels. They finally brought us home.

I know it sounds extremely simplistic, but from that day forward, our lives were completely changed. We started every day with Jesus. We prayed, and life became bigger than ourselves. As a couple, we never questioned our commitment. We were on the same track, growing together in God.

Pastor John Maxwell was wise and realized that Phil and I were clueless in understanding the Bible. He wanted us to know what we believed and who we believed in. A mature couple from the church mentored us on a weekly basis through the book of John. John gives a bedrock foundation for who Jesus Christ says he is – the Son of God, from the beginning to the end of time.

During this process, God gently, lovingly opened my eyes to my sins – adultery, divorce, selfishness, pride, deception, immorality, carelessness – not only with others, but also with myself. I realized everything I had been doing was a sin. Blaming my brother for something he didn't do in third grade, lying to my parents in seventh grade, my rudeness to my parents, my sexual promiscuity, my drinking, my gossip, my envy, my lying – *so* much lying. Not only was my behavior sinful, but so were my thoughts. Anything that doesn't glorify God is sin.

Finally, I realized *everyone* is a sinner. Not one person can stand blameless before God. He is holy, and the only way to stand before Him is to have our sins forgiven. The solution to this is Jesus. He came to earth as a man and took our place, dying on the cross as punishment for our sin. He rose again and conquered death, making a way for us to spend eternity with Him in heaven. Jesus filled the empty hole deep down in my soul, and I realized I did not have to fear death. Since I trusted in Jesus and his sacrifice, I was washed clean by his blood. I was finally beginning to get it! All of this was true for me and is true for anyone who believes.

Pastor Maxwell had a friend named Josh McDowell who further grounded us in the person of Jesus and his word. Josh and his wife, Dotti, lived on the Campus Crusade property in the mountains east of San Diego in a town called Julian. They hosted events for college students.

Josh's journey to Jesus began with doubt. He was a huge skeptic. A college girl challenged him by saying that Christianity was not about religion but about a relationship with Jesus Christ. Josh set out to disprove Christianity and dove into it like a prosecuting attorney. After studying ancient historical records, manuscripts, eyewitness accounts, and archaeological evidence, he could no longer deny who Jesus was – the Son of God who came to take away the sin of the world. From then on, he developed a passion to make sure people knew, without a doubt, who Jesus was.

Pastor Maxwell suggested we join others in a seminar called Six Hours with Josh, an intense program led by Josh McDowell that took place over a Friday and Saturday. He had the energy of a teenager, and it was easy to absorb all the facts that he brought forward. For the first time in my life, I understood the meaning of Christmas and Easter.

By May, Phil and I stood on solid ground. We knew who and what we believed in. Jesus was our foundation, and boy, were we going to need it! Like any newly married couple, we had no idea of the trials and struggles to come in the years ahead, but our faith was never shaken.

Phil and I approached Pastor Maxwell about being baptized together. We set the date for June 30, 1985, six months after Jesus met us at the door of our church.

It was a glorious Sunday. We were in the water together, and Pastor Maxwell asked each one of us if Jesus Christ was the Lord of our lives. Of course, the answer was yes! As I went under the water for those brief seconds, I knew my past had been completely washed away. For both Phil and me, this was a new beginning. We knew that heaven was our eternal home.

That day brought Phil and I even closer. After years of never being satisfied and always searching, we were grounded in a marriage with Jesus at the center. To the very depths of my soul, I knew that Phil and I were united till death do us part.

Phil and I truly wanted children. During all my years of wanton immorality, it was a miracle I never got pregnant. Phil and I had stopped using birth control over two years prior and had already begun infertility treatment. At this point, I was already thirty-six years old. My doctor, Dr. Q, dealt specifically with older women and endocrinology. Back then, infertility treatments were nothing like they are today. After two failed attempts, Dr. Q said there wasn't much more he could do.

Infertility was a huge problem amongst my fellow flight attendants. We weren't really sure why – maybe it was the crazy schedule or the ups and downs of take-offs and landings – but it was a common issue. In hopes of getting pregnant, I chose to back off of flying. I went to work in the flight attendant training department with a normal Monday to Friday schedule.

I really enjoyed this new job. PSA had a brand-new facility at Scripps Ranch, northeast of downtown San Diego. All flight attendants, pilots, and crew members had to complete yearly recurrent training. Entire cabins and cockpits were constructed for simulations with all sorts of programmed scenarios, from extreme weather to airplane malfunctions. One year, they even took us through an actual decompression along with a mock water landing. I was shocked at how quickly one becomes silly and uncoordinated when deprived of oxygen! Working on the training end, I made sure my students realized how vitally important their role was while also encouraging them to have fun and love their jobs.

In late August, I started having horrible cramps and spotting. On September 17, I finally got in to see Dr. Q.

The nurse examined my urine sample and called Dr. Q out of the room. He returned, grinning from ear to ear.

"Well, nothing we did worked, but you are definitely pregnant!"

Due to the heavy bleeding, he wanted an ultrasound. I was a mess of emotions, all the way from sheer joy to absolute terror. As much as we wanted a baby, I had no clue what to do with one! I had been such a horrible, rotten teenager. The neighborhood moms had never asked me to babysit; I'd never even changed a diaper, nor had Phil!

Once Phil had arrived at the doctor's office and absorbed that I was pregnant, we were ready for the ultrasound – the first of many. Phil held my hand. He stared at me, then stared at the monitor, stared at me, stared at the monitor. We were in complete shock, but what came next sent us over the edge.

The technician added more of the ice-cold gel to her ultrasound wand.

"Well, I see one heartbeat."

She continued to swirl her wand around.

"And I see another one. You're having twins."

We burst into laughter, followed by tears, followed by pure joy. She continued in a quiet voice.

"One of the heartbeats is very faint. I want the doctor to come in and look."

After Dr. Q observed the two teeny tiny beeps on the monitor, he asked us to come into his office. We all sat down.

"It appears you are about nine weeks pregnant with a due date around March 25. However, one of the heartbeats is so faint that we feel you may lose that baby. The other baby should be fine and finish out the pregnancy. Of course, due to your age, we'll keep a close eye on you and monitor you frequently. To try to save baby B and due to your bleeding, I want you to go home for complete bed rest over the next two weeks. You might want to get the wheels in motion for a medical leave from work. I'll write the orders so you can give it to the airline."

He was a little emotional as he said congratulations again and that he'd see us in two weeks for another ultrasound.

It was already late in the afternoon when we left the doctor's office.

"I'm starving," Phil said. "Let's go home so you can put your feet up and I'll go get us some dinner."

While he was gone, I got out my calendar. He walked in with dinner about forty minutes later.

"Well, we were baptized on June 30," I said, "and I got pregnant very soon after. We need to tease Pastor Maxwell that whatever he put in that water, it worked!"

We laughed until we cried. We were frightened for the next two weeks but full of joy for what was to come.

The waiting was like hell – lying there, only getting up for food and to go to the bathroom, not knowing if baby B was alive or dead. Every morning and night, Phil prayed over me and for baby A and baby B, especially baby B.

Two weeks later, we were back in the technician's room for our ultrasound. Once again, she swirled around the wand with the ice-cold gel, looking for heart-beats.

Phil and I were both too afraid to look into each other's eyes. Would our prayers be answered? As we waited, Phil sat on one of those padded stools with wheels. He leaned toward me and wrapped his left arm around my head, his right hand squeezing the blood out of mine.

We held our breath.

Finally, the technician spoke.

"I see one heartbeat."

Silence. She kept swirling.

"And, I see two heartbeats. Congratulations, you are having twins!"

We both broke into tears of unbelievable joy. Our prayers had been answered!

Someone showed me Psalm 139 in the Bible. This passage told of how the God of the universe knew me personally. He knew when I sat and when I laid down. He went before me and knew it all. Even when there was darkness that overwhelmed me and I was scared, He was there and made it bright as day. Not only did He know me, but He was forming my babies in my womb. In their secret, safe, warm, and protected place, they were being gloriously knitted together. He knew my babies and the number of their days even before they had seen the light of day. I was in awe at what was taking place inside of me!

Doctor Q wanted me to stay on bedrest for a few more weeks. The remainder of the pregnancy went just as God planned it. The babies stayed in the same positions almost the entire pregnancy. Baby A hogged the entire womb while baby B was curled up under my ribs. Baby A was definitely a boy, and we thought baby B was a girl. We have an ultrasound picture of baby B trying to stretch out her legs while her bully brother kicked her back up under my ribs. As soon as I was able, we headed up the coast to the Coliseum. The twins attended their first USC football games before they were even born.

After the initial bedrest, my only issue during pregnancy came in the last month when the babies finally shifted positions. They were both feet down. In the last few weeks, I reached 205 pounds. My toes looked like individual sausages, and my ankles resembled my upper thighs.

On March 20, five days before my due date, my water broke at 4:00 a.m. I took a shower, washed my hair, passed on putting on my make-up, then woke Phil.

By then the contractions were coming regularly.

Due to the babies being feet down, we already knew I was going to have a C-section. The operating room was full of the surgical crew. Phil was scrubbed. I was prepped and looked up at the anesthesiologist.

"When are they going to begin?" I asked.

He laughed.

"Baby A is already on his way out!"

Isn't local anesthesia awesome? It was 7:29 a.m.

"All right, now for our girl!"

Everyone in the room gasped. Our second baby was delivered at 7:31 a.m., and it was another boy!

Phil and I both began to cry. We named the babies Matthew and Mark. After the deliveries, I went to sleep under those fabulous, heated blankets. Phil held the boys for the first two hours of their lives. What miracles they were!

Since I was a high-risk case, my insurance scheduled my hospital stay for five days. Remember, much of my adult life had been spent in beautiful hotels and resorts. I was thinking I had five days of rest to enjoy myself! I'd never babysat or changed a diaper – ever.

The next morning, the nurse wheeled the boys into the room.

"All right, honey, time to change these boys' diapers!" she said cheerfully.

Oh, I hope I meet this nurse again one day to apologize profusely for what I said next. In my mind, I had a five-day reservation with maid and diaper service, like a resort.

"Excuse me," I said. "I have another four days here. I don't have to change them yet."

Oh, the look this precious, hard-working, wonderful nurse gave me!

"Honey, get your butt outta that bed and start changing these diapers!"

Please, Lord, let me see her in heaven so I can apologize!

POSTPARTUM DEPRESSION

If someone had said to me, "You know, the next six weeks might be hard," I probably would've wanted to slap them first and then push them off a cliff.

I remained totally clueless as I recovered from my C-section and began caring for two babies. Phil was as exhausted as I was, but he never complained. He probably felt like there was no point. There was nothing we could do about it. I, however, had different thoughts.

Mark had horrible colic, and it only flared up after we'd gone to bed and fallen asleep.

Then, it began – he started crying, becoming nearly hysterical until his daddy picked him up and walked him around for what seemed like hours.

Phil placed Mark face down across his forearm with pressure on his tummy, Mark straddling his arm like a tree limb. After a while, Mark was soothed enough to only emit faint groans that occasionally erupted into loud wails of agony. The hours ticked away. Finally, Phil was able to put Mark back in the crib, snuggled up with his brother Matt. Phil grabbed a few hours of sleep before showering and heading off to work. This went on for three weeks straight. It would be safe to presume we both resembled the cast from *The Night of the Living Dead.*

For days on end, the boys were on opposite schedules. One slept while the other was awake. One had colic all night and the other cried all day. One wouldn't nurse and the other took it all. One was constipated and the other had projectile diarrhea. I can't even talk about trying to breastfeed both of them at the same time! The only living being that was at peace through all of the chaos was Shannon, our family Labrador Retriever. She adored the boys and slept blissfully under their crib. I, on the other hand, was a zombie.

Late one afternoon, Phil found me wandering around outside, still in my robe. Our front door was wide open, and both boys were inside the house, screaming. He gently put his arm around me and guided me back toward the house.

"Honey, why are you out here? Let's go inside."

I placed my head in my hands.

"I left the door open hoping someone would come and take them."

He suggested I call Dr. Q the next day.

I got a late afternoon appointment, and the receptionist guided me into Dr. Q's office. I was right at five weeks post-delivery. I sat down and started sobbing, telling him I couldn't handle this. He was a gentle, wise man who just listened. I took a deep breath and revealed my deepest thoughts to him between sobs.

"I know we went to a lot of trouble to have these babies, but…do you know anyone who might want them?"

My thoughts were out there. I waited for his response.

"Sandee, you and Phil did exactly as you pleased for years. You traveled, skied, vacationed, went on cruises, went to the theatre; of course, this lifestyle change is a huge shock. You don't have to feel like you love these babies. Next week is your six-week check-up. Come back then and we'll talk about this and see what we can do."

The freedom to say what was truly on my heart was exactly what I needed. Dr. Q's validation of my feelings and his desire to discuss them next week brought a huge release to me, and Phil was relieved when things calm down a bit.

The next week, Dr. Q and I once again sat across from each other in his office. He held my hands and asked how I was.

"We've decided to keep them!" I responded joyfully.

We talked some more on a deep, serious level. He had hoped that the freedom to say how I felt, as horrible as it was, would set my hormones into motion to get back on track. That's exactly what it did. Back then, postpartum depression wasn't diagnosed as readily as it is now. I'm thankful that I had a doctor who listened to me and was ready to get Phil and family more involved if needed. Postpartum depression is very real. If you are struggling, please let someone know and seek help.

Six weeks after the delivery, Phil and I snuck out for a date night. We reminisced about the delivery, and we both were wondering the answer to the same question.

"Why did you start crying when you realized it was another boy and not a girl?"

Neither one of us wanted to say. Finally, I blurted out my feelings.

"Because I was such a lying, conniving, rotten girl. I did not want to raise someone like me!"

Phil confessed that because of the teasing he got from his sisters, he wanted nothing to do with girls. Both of us were ecstatic to have two boys.

BABA

From the moment I met Phil, he told me he'd always take care of his mom. I knew this was non-negotiable, but I never dreamt it would lead to what was coming next.

When I was trying to get pregnant, we assumed we would soon move out of our condo and into a home. Phil approached me with what he thought was a brilliant idea. He poured us two glasses of wine and started to make his case.

"At some point, Mom will end up moving in with us. Do we want to just clear out a bedroom where she will feel like she is an intrusion or..." He took a deep breath, a sip of his red wine, and continued. "...what if she sold her Emerald Bay place and we all went in on building a house with a view? She could have her section and we could have ours. She'd be with us, but not on top of us."

He stared at me, waiting. I honestly don't remember how long I sat there or what went through my mind, but I took a deep breath and said, "Let's do it."

We found a vacant lot east of I-5 on a steep hill. It had a great view of Mission Bay, all the way from SeaWorld to Mount Soledad. It was located in a post-WWII neighborhood with small homes, most lots being only fifty feet wide. We drew up a plan. The living areas and bedrooms faced Mission Bay. The house was tiered in three levels, and each one had a gorgeous view. There was no yard – just multiple levels of decks and a steep cliff.

Right when I found out I was pregnant, we broke ground and construction began. Our hopes were to move in before the babies arrived. Of course, construction never goes as planned, so we eventually had a move-in date of mid-June. The boys would be 3 months old.

By this time, I had several flight attendant friends who were also mothers. All of them hired women who came up from Tijuana to watch their babies while they flew. One afternoon, I received a call from one of my friends who knew I was soon to deliver and would be looking for help. For eight years, a woman from Tijuana named Natalia had lived with them. Their daughter was now of the age where she no longer needed Natalia, but they couldn't bring themselves to just let her go; she truly was a member of their family. We met Natalia. She spoke no English, but Phil's mom spoke Spanish with ease. Together, we figured out Natalia was around fifty years old.

A few weeks after delivery, she came over. She held the boys, and her soft round arms wrapped them in love. We knew we had found a treasure. For five years, Natalia came up on Sunday night or early Monday morning and returned to Tijuana on Friday. She didn't cook, but she helped clean and, of course, took care of the babies. During the time she lived with us, we were her sponsors and helped her get a permanent resident card. The boys adored her. Between both she and my mother-in-law joining our family, we had the most loving environment that I could imagine for our boys.

My life was now such a long way from my days of just walking out on whatever didn't make me happy. Was I happy? I was beyond exhausted and overwhelmed. But to the depths of my soul, I had a peace that was pure and indescribable. I was so in love with Phil, and he adored me and his boys so very much.

Even though I was full of joy and peace, nothing was easy. Phil and I went from just the two of us doing as we pleased to four of us to *six* of us in the blink of an eye. Somehow, we adjusted.

One day shortly after we moved into the house, Phil was driving to work listening to *Focus on the Family* on the radio. The show that day was about family dynamics, and someone mentioned that two women shouldn't live under the same roof.

What have I done? he thought immediately.

He must have felt the tension building between my mother-in-law and myself. Her way of doing things in the kitchen was not my way, and she let me know. It was the same stress with laundry, feedings, and meals. All of this made me feel inadequate.

God worked in our hearts in a miraculous way. The "old" me – the one who only cared about myself and only wanted to be happy – would have bailed out on Phil and his mom, probably even the boys, and said, "Adios!" Instead, we worked it out. My sweet, wonderful husband had the three of us sit down every few months and just talk things out. There was always something that was grating on one of us, but Phil guided us back to neutral ground and peace. Never once did I tell Phil that he had to choose between her or me. That right there is enough for me to know God can take a selfish heart and change it for the good!

For sixteen years, his mom and I were together. We battled for supremacy, but we made it through grace, forgiveness, laughter, prayer, and talks. I loved her and, in due time, she loved me. We all called her Baba.

Three months after the boys were born, I was down from my 205 pounds and back into my uniforms. The five-day work week of the training department was too hectic for us, so I went back to flying. Fortunately, I had a lot of seniority, so I was able to bid flights that worked around our new family and Phil's schedule.

Plus, one of the babies had an upcoming surgery for a heart condition.

Nothing is more difficult or heart wrenching than handing a tiny baby over to a nurse to take into a heart surgery operating room. It was one of the most difficult things Phil or I ever had to do. However, we had so many people praying for us and praying for our baby that we had a peace and comfort that I can't explain. The next nine months were a blur as we focused on the boys and their care.

When the boys were born, I started keeping journals.

5/19/1987
The surgery was very successful, and the prayers were many. Thank you, Jesus, the prayers were heard. He is one happy, healthy, beautiful boy. They both are such a tremendous joy to us, oh Lord. Lord, I pray you give Phil and I the will to bring them up as men of God with a joyful heart and laughing eyes – like their daddy.

OUR BOYS

After my brief postpartum depression period was over and we decided to keep the boys, we actually grew pretty fond of them. Obviously, this is a huge joke in our family now. Words cannot describe the joy that they brought to us.

Once, Phil was the speaker at a large dinner for the Professional Convention Management Association (PCMA). As he began to speak, he pulled a pacifier out of his coat pocket; he didn't know he'd left it there the week prior. He got a bit emotional as he held it up in front of this group of 2,000 people.

"There's a part of your heart that is not unlocked until you have a child."

Those who had known him for years saw a changed person right before their eyes.

We called the boys the rolling monkeys. They were constantly rolling around on the floor, wrestling each other, giggling, and snuggling. Having a twin brother was the best – a forever friend. People may think having twins would be incredibly difficult, but we thought it was easy because we never knew anything else. Changing one diaper? Might as well change two! The boys had the same friends and were always on the same sports teams, so we only had one set of practices and games to attend. The boys had a great life full of traveling, jumping on Mom's airplanes, and staying at Dad's hotels.

Phil and I had the same thoughts and worries as every parent. Would the boys grow and develop at the right rates per the charts? Would they have struggles at school that we wouldn't be aware of, maybe with a coach, a teacher, or friends? And most importantly, would they come to know Jesus as their own Savior, not just Mom and Dad's God?

Phil and I worked our travel schedules around each other so that one of us was always home with the boys. Many nights we were all home together and ended up in their rooms, on our knees beside their beds. Before going to sleep, we had two short songs we all sang; one was about casting all of our cares upon God and the other was about the plan that God had for our lives. Then we prayed over our precious sons, for Jesus to watch over them, guide them in all that they did, and for them to trust Jesus as their Lord and Savior. The moment they were born, we began praying for their future wives, for women who would love Jesus and our boys with all their hearts and laugh a ton. Many years later, our prayers were answered!

As the boys got older, their teenage years were easy. We knew all of their friends' parents; they were always baffled by the underground network of moms.

They never figured out how we knew stuff! But Matt and Mark were great boys. We were not fraught with concerns about who they were with or what they were doing. They had both proven they could make sound decisions regarding friends, and they always called us if they were going from one friend's house to another. Our home was full of an abundance of love, hugs, kisses, rules, boundaries, and trust. The words "I'm sorry" weren't just reserved for the boys; Phil and I apologized often, too.

Little by little, Phil and I revealed our past to them. When I questioned them about where they were going or who they were playing with, they'd laugh and say, "Mom, we are nothing like you!"

True, they were not. What an answer to prayer!

WHY WAIT?

Pastor John Maxwell and Josh McDowell had great ideas and wanted to partner with Phil. They had been planning two separate events, but the details had not come together. A lot of loose ends were dangling.

In 1986, San Diego had not yet attracted the major convention hotels. Phil was such a talented businessman and marketing person, and one of his hotels had the only convention space in town. He was the perfect fit to join up with these two amazing men and help form the events. The first one was called Quest '86, and the purpose to reach the business community for Christ. The other was called Why Wait, and its purpose was to reach teens in regard to sex and why they should wait – or not. The plans for both events were thrown into motion.

Pastor Maxwell truly had a passion to help others and make a difference in people's lives. With Quest '86, he wanted to reach businesspeople who didn't think they needed Christ. These people were self-sufficient, well-to-do members of society, totally fine on their own. Why did they need God? John, Josh, and Phil reached out to Christ-centered men and women in the community to be speakers and promoters. They gathered attorneys, judges, doctors, newscasters, and players from the San Diego Padres and Chargers. These promoters invited everyone they knew. They advertised the upcoming event on the radio and in newspapers. The event was held at the convention center of the Town and Country Hotel with more than 1,000 people in attendance. Phil certainly was not the party animal out of N'awlins anymore.

We got in on the Why Wait campaign during its infancy. Josh and his wife, Dottie, invited seven or so mature Christian couples up to their property in the mountains east of San Diego. Why were we included? Only God knows! The boys were only six months old. When we arrived, they were quickly snatched up by giggling teenage girls who whisked them off to the campus nursery.

Josh explained the timeline for the kick-off. He also had the idea of running a contest for students ages twelve to nineteen. To enter, they had to write an essay on why they waited to have sex or why they didn't. I think the prize was some incredible sound system. The essays from this contest eventually became the substance of a book Josh wrote on the subject.

I was fairly skeptical. From the comments pouring forth from those around the table, it was clear that they had all made up their minds that sex should be saved for marriage. I knew from my past that if someone had told me to wait, the idea would have gotten zero traction with me. How in the world did they expect to reach teenagers and get them to talk about sex if they'd already made up their minds? I knew I had to start praying about this, and I did.

In February of 1987, Josh McDowell invited eighty people to attend a larger Why Wait meeting. Phil and I hosted, and we met in our living room. Josh stood up by our fireplace and laid out his entire dream about capturing the pulse of teen sexuality and gaining ground toward God.

God had answered my prayers; I now clearly saw his perfect plan for marriage. During my teen and young adult years, I had been so promiscuous and off-course. No marriage could have survived when my primary motivation was just being happy. I learned so much from Josh about why I had always been searching for love in all the wrong places. I had such a deep hole in my heart that only Jesus could fill. My ex-husbands had all told me they loved me, and, as far as I knew, my dad had loved me, too. But none of them were able to give me the love and confidence I needed. I spent my childhood idolizing the strong, protective Ben Cartwright from *Bonanza* and Matt Dillon from *Gunsmoke*, but now I realized that the solution to my emptiness was Jesus. He was now my strength and had given me a sweet peace, confidence, and joy. Plus, he'd blessed me with a strong, protective husband to grow old with!

Why Wait went on to be a huge campaign and the book has ministered to hundreds of thousands of teens and parents worldwide. Phil and I were so blessed to be a part of it!

My mom often came over from Arizona to cuddle with her precious grandbabies. When she was in town, she went to church with us. One Sunday, she leaned over and whispered to me, "I believe in Jesus, and I want to be prayed over." Oh my, how my heart leapt out of my chest! Mom was baptized in our pool in May of 1989. In 2003, she was called to heaven. I know she is there right now, walking the streets of gold. I cannot wait to hug her, forever.

God had given Phil and me a marriage that delighted our hearts. This giant of a man was so gentle and loved me and his boys so very much. Phil was profoundly affected by his dad's death when he was only eight years old. I wrote about this in my journal.

6/21/87

Phil's biggest fear is that he'll die when the boys are eight, just like his dad. I know Lord, he would give up his life just to see Mark and Matt through high school. I pray Lord Jesus You let him see M and M till they're grown men – or Your will...whatever comes first!

Little did we know how profound this journal entry would be in seven years.

But little do we ever know what the next breath will bring.

On December 7, 1987, PSA Flight 1771 took off with thirty-eight passengers and five crew members on board, including a man named David Burke, a disgruntled employee who had just been terminated. Also onboard was his terminating boss, Ray Thompson.

David went into the bathroom and came out with a .44 Magnum revolver. He shot Thompson twice. The First Officer immediately radioed in that shots had been fired. Flight attendant Debra Neil rushed into the cockpit.

"We have a problem," she said.

"What's the problem?" the captain responded.

"I'm the problem."

David Burke had entered the cockpit. He shot the flight attendant and both pilots.

He then pushed the control column and forced the plane into a dive. It crashed into a field near Cayucos, California, and killed everyone on board. The National Transportation Safety Board learned that Burke had been fired for stealing $69.00 from cocktail receipts and some other petty thefts.

The description of this event may sound like I'm a distant reporter, but these were my friends, people I had flown with for years. When I think about it, it makes my heart ache with painful memories. Up until 1987, employees were still able to easily bypass security by showing their airline badges. In response to this crash, this was no longer allowed, and employees were required to immediately surrender their credentials upon termination, resignation, or retirement.

Life can change – or end – more quickly than we would ever like to imagine.

ANYWHERE BUT NEW YORK

Phil was known as a leader and a futurist in the hotel, convention, and meeting industry. In the mid-80s, sales departments still tracked leads and potential customers using paper trails, stuffing file cabinets full of information. These systems were full of logistical problems. What the heck was in all of the drawers? How can a person know where anything is or if the information is current? Phil was always thinking of ways to do business better. We discussed him venturing out on his own and made it a reality.

Over the next three years, Phil created Data Comm, a consulting company that used computer software to digitize client bases. This company was eventually sold to Bill Communications. Starting a business is extremely difficult. Our life was full of spikes of exhilaration followed by dive bombs into dead ends and drained finances. However, Phil gradually saw some traction take hold with technology. Spreadsheets slowly began to replace paper files, but not all companies bought into it. They didn't trust computers when they could hold paper in their hands.

The mid-80s was also a time when smaller airlines were being gobbled up by larger ones. Sadly, my PSA was one of them. In 1988, PSA merged with USAir. (And in 2013, USAir merged with American Airlines.) This merge changed so many things about my career.

Almost immediately, USAir closed the San Diego crew base, so I had to drive to Los Angeles to check in for my flights. The East Coast had a much better selection, so many of my friends put their homes on the market and moved to a massive international crew base in Charlotte, North Carolina. They were able to purchase huge, beautiful homes on Lake Norman for a third of what their homes sold for in San Diego.

The merge was both exciting and depressing at the same time. PSA had carved a niche on the West Coast. Many people only flew PSA; our uniforms, our humor, our customer service, and our air fares made us unique. It seemed like USAir wanted to change everything that PSA excelled at. During the essential but also boring oxygen demonstration, we were no longer allowed to drop a rubber chicken instead of the oxygen mask or tell the smoking passengers they had to step outside onto the wing. There was no more humor or joking over the PA system, and no more teasing the passengers. We were professionals now.

USAir even wanted to bring their East Coast style of food into our galleys. They brought in ovens so we could serve breakfasts of bacon, sausages, and eggs rather than our signature fresh fruit and bagels. Instead of our avocado and chicken salad lunch, they brought in pastrami and corned beef sandwiches. Passengers revolted. They flocked to a fairly new carrier out of Texas that initially struggled on the West Coast – Southwest Airlines. It wasn't long before the vast majority of flights up and down the West Coast started going to Southwest. USAir flights out of Los Angeles no longer went up and down the coast; they only flew to the East Coast and back. My flight choices were becoming exceedingly limited.

Phil felt that California was too laid back for the business ideas he had. He wanted to be where the action was, where more futuristic thinkers were. He just knew someone had to be interested in him and his concepts. (I was just praying he would make some money!) From the East Coast, there were much better flying routes – even some to Europe. We began entertaining the idea of moving.

Even though Phil had sold his technology company for only pennies on the dollar, he wasn't ready to go back into the regular business world. He had a pioneer spirit regarding technology, but he truly was before his time. Unfortunately, it wasn't paying the bills. We were down to the last $19.00 in our checking account and couldn't pay the mortgage. We had to sell the house, but where would we go?

One night, we were sitting in our jacuzzi overlooking Mission Bay.

"Honey, I'll go anywhere with you but New York," I said.

I'm not sure why I said this. Perhaps New York just sounded too bazaar, too much of a change for this laid-back Southern California beach girl. I knew God would use our story and our changed lives wherever we ended up, but I was praying that it wouldn't be New York.

Guess where we moved?

The house overlooking Mission Bay sold quickly. Phil and I were shocked when Baba willingly chose to leave her beloved Southern California roots and move with us. We thought she'd choose to move back to Laguna Beach, into a garden home near all of her friends. But her attachment to her two rambunctious grandsons was too strong.

The hardest part about pulling up our California roots was leaving Natalia behind. We drove her home to Tijuana one last time. After many, many hugs and kisses, we had to literally pull wet-faced and runny-nosed Matt and Mark off her neck. We all sobbed as we drove away and headed north, back across the Tijuana border for the last time.

5/23/92

Our new address as of July 24, 1992, will be 4012 Park Ave, Edison, New Jersey. A 45-minute Amtrak commute for Phil into New York City – XYZ Hotel Corporate headquarters! I'll be based out of Philadelphia, a 90-minute drive south on the NJ Turnpike. Lord, You take us where we don't want to go and turn it into Your glory! Two California beach kids taking the train into NYC and the turnpike to Philadelphia!

Phil's new job was heading up XYZ Hotel's National Sales department. Every day, Phil took the Amtrak train into the heart of New York City. I used the New Jersey Turnpike to get to my new Philadelphia crew base. We found a great home close to the train station and the elementary school. It had a great master bedroom on the main floor for Baba and an additional bedroom for us upstairs.

The stark contrast from the West Coast to the East Coast was thrilling. Phil and I were like two kids in a candy store. New York City! About two weeks after arriving in New Jersey, we had our first date night.

We drove our huge, bright red Dodge Caravan north on I-95 and across the George Washington Bridge, over the Hudson River. I was exhilarated by the history that was all around us. In 1776, General George Washington had crossed the Hudson River – the same river we were driving over – during the Revolutionary War. In 1804, Alexander Hamilton was shot by Aaron Burr on a bluff above the river. Everywhere we turned, there was history!

The bright lights of New York City wrapped around our van along with hundreds of yellow taxi cabs. I had never seen so many taxis in my life! The only other cars amidst this sea of yellow appeared to be black limos. Then there was our bright red Dodge Caravan, too tall to fit in any garage. We giggled at the novelty of everything and drove in circles until we finally found a parking spot. We held each other's hands tightly, our excitement and giddiness fueled by this intoxicating city that lit up the night sky. We wandered around for hours.

Finally, we settled into a little pub off of Times Square. We sat on bar stools, just like a couple of locals – only we weren't. Hopefully, we weren't too obvious. We tried to look cool and nonchalant. Arm in arm, we eventually wandered back to our van. Thankfully, it still had all four tires. We had joked that our soccer mom van was probably being stripped while we enjoyed a cold beer. I guess it wasn't tire theft material.

We drove back across the George Washington, south on I-95, got off at Exit 10, and went home. The house was quiet, and we tiptoed up the stairs to peek in on the boys. Their beds were empty. Of course, we found them cuddled up in the middle of our bed instead. Life was good.

No, life was *great*.

The boys were now six years old. They adored their Baba and often piled into her room with our dog and two cats to watch TV. They adjusted easily to their new school and found some fabulous friends, as did I. Phil was never home; his new job was eating him up, so he had to live through my stories of what life was like in our New Jersey neighborhood. We also kept our USC season football tickets, and for our first two years in New Jersey we enjoyed the beauty of our two careers – my airline passes and Phil's hotel rooms – and flew out to Los Angeles for most home games. Over time, however, school and their activities started to take precedent.

I started work at my new Philadelphia crew base. Gone were my close flight attendant and crew friends. My flirty colorful uniform had been replaced with a navy-blue business suit with either a skirt or pants paired with a white shirt. There was no color or flair, but we were professional. I was ready for my first trip.

I walked into a huge crew lounge, and no one appeared to know each other. I finally found a few crew members that would be on my first four-day trip. Once we got on board, we introduced ourselves to the rest of the crew. The lead flight attendant was all business and no fun – I was told where to go, where to sit, which side of the plane to work, and that was it. For now, I was the low man on the totem pole.

9/28/92

Phil is working very long hours – in the morning he is gone by 6:30 and home after boys are in bed at 7:30. Lord, I know this is for a reason. You didn't bring us to NJ so Phil would be gone 13 hours a day unless it is Your will and part of Your plan! We feel in our hearts that a year from now things will be different as Your plan unfolds. Lord, You have protected our family and marriage thus far, and we pray for your continued protection. Bind us in Your care. Help us to find a new church home so we, Baba, and the boys can be grounded and continue to grow in You Lord. Well, I'm off to find Vietnamese food here in San Francisco. This is my first trip on a 757 with a Philadelphia-based crew. I love You, Lord.

The vast majority of people seeking a place to worship in New Jersey were either Catholic or Muslim, so finding a Protestant church was not easy. They were few and far between, but we found a great one and quickly became involved. In May of 1993, I found myself going to my first women's retreat.

While there, the Lord used all my past hurts, pains, and blunders to minister to two young women. I hadn't yet shared my past with anyone in New Jersey, but for some reason they came to talk to me. They asked if there was any difference between a marriage with no faith in God and one that had something – Jesus – holding it together. I was dumbfounded. Why had they approached me?

"Yes!" I stammered out, and shared about all of my failures, from a life only focused on myself to sobbing on the Las Vegas hotel floor, crying out to a God

I didn't know. The picture of the three-cord strand came to mind. I shared with them how God had given me my heart's desire and love in Phil.

5/23/93

Sweet Jesus, you are the glue. You are the third cord that twists around us to keep us together and won't let us unravel. I can't imagine You not being in the midst of all our discussions, especially family matters. I can't imagine handing our baby over for heart surgery without the church praying for him or for us. I can't imagine You not being part of Phil's business decisions or our move. My getting along with Baba – right there is a miracle! Thank You Jesus for being with us!

6/15/93

Tampa, FL. My sweet Lord, Your majesty was so obvious this morning as I took a long walk along a beautiful inlet. The water, the early morning sun dancing through palm trees, ferns and Spanish moss – this is a tropical wonderland. In New Jersey, we have the splendor of the seasons, rich garden soil, green everywhere plus huge trees. Your creation Father is beyond comprehension...and to think that Heaven is far greater than anything here. WOW!

1/2/94

PARIS! I am the lead flight attendant on this crew. Lord, I can't believe it!!! I am flying first class to Paris in charge of my own 757! From 16 take-offs and landings up and down the California coast in one day to a three-day trip to Paris! International-al flights are so much more detailed; the paperwork, customs, the food service, wine service, movies...it is amazing how everything fits! This schedule works perfect for the boys and Phil...I check in late Thursday afternoon, land in Paris Friday morning, take a nap, and get up and explore. A girl I flew with took me to a 6:30 p.m. mass at Notre Dame! Now I'm on an island in the middle of the Seine River. Absolutely gorgeous! I am fading fast (jet lag) and must get sleep.

On June 17, 1994, our entire family was glued to the TV in Baba's room. A news helicopter chased after a white Ford Bronco traveling slowly on a Los Angeles freeway. O.J. Simpson was sitting in the back seat. The boys were fascinated because O.J. was the famous USC running back who had won the Heisman Trophy in 1968. For Baba, a lifelong devoted USC Trojan, the claims they were making against O.J. couldn't possibly be true.

After all, O.J. was a USC Trojan.

THE PHONE CALL

Working in New York City was exciting, but Phil being away from us for twelve to fourteen hours every day was a huge downside. It started to take a toll on his health, both mentally and physically.

I suggested he look for another job, something not as stressful and closer to home. We had grown much stronger in our faith. We tried not to react on impulse but instead tried to seek God's direction. I tended to react; in contrast, Phil was the calming force, the safe port in a storm. He said we weren't going to move or make any decisions until we prayed and sought God's direction for our lives. We decided to wait and see if other opportunities came up at XYZ. In the meantime, Phil decided to go to the doctor for a physical. He just was not feeling up to speed.

The next week, XYZ flew Phil to Chicago for his yearly review. They informed him they no longer needed him in New York City, but they had a great opportunity in the Midwest – another move. The thought of telling me made him sick to his stomach. He arrived home that night and noticed a few drops of blood in his urine. He chalked it up to stress. He still hadn't scheduled his physical.

We started praying about what was next with XYZ and our family. Phil was extremely focused on seeking God's will and specifically asked that all doors be closed that were not from him.

Over the next month, it became clear that XYZ and Phil did not fit together in their business philosophies, and Phil resigned. He didn't fear the process of finding another job. He had a reputation in the hotel and convention industry. Finally, it was a good time to schedule his physical.

Afterward, he met with Dr. Murphy who wanted him to get a bladder biopsy. The outpatient procedure was scheduled for the next day. Neither of us talked about it; we didn't think it was anything major. A few days later, Dr. Murphy called with the results.

The bladder biopsy revealed Phil had cancer.

What? It couldn't be. My big, strong, godly man – with cancer?

The doctor explained that this particular cancer was deadly, with a survival rate of only 18%. Few lived past twelve months.

We prayed. The boys were so young. We couldn't imagine a life for them without their dad. They adored him, and Phil loved them beyond words. He often talked about how his love for them was only a fraction of the love God has for us. Why was this happening to us?

The next week was a blur of tests and CT scans. Surgery was scheduled for just two weeks later, on July 12, 1994. I rearranged my flights to have two weeks off to help with Phil's recovery. In the meantime, I had one trip left to Paris.

After an uneventful flight, I headed to the hotel and took my usual mid-morning nap. Afterward, I set out for my walk and ended up by the Seine River. I picked up a tiny loaf of bread, some cheese, a Pellegrino water, and a fruit tart from the bakery. I sat there and watched couples stroll along the river with their arms around each other. My heart was back home with Phil. I stared at the river current flowing past me and prayed. I prayed that God would give Phil's body the strength he needed to get through the surgery. I prayed for the doctor and surgical team, that they would have wisdom and discernment. I prayed for God to cleanse Phil and take the cancer from his body.

It was summertime in Paris, and a warm romantic evening settled in. I couldn't have cared less. I headed back to the hotel exhausted, longing for a good night's sleep.

So many people were praying for Phil and his surgery, including our new church family in New Jersey and our former church family in San Diego. My twelve-year-old niece flew in to keep the boys company and to help Baba care for them. During surgery, our pastor came and sat with me.

The surgery lasted four hours, and they removed two thirds of Phil's bladder as well as a bunch of lymph nodes. After it was over, the nurse told us that Phil had gone into the operating room singing praise songs and praying for the doctor.

"God is not done with that man yet," our pastor said, laughing. "He has great things in store for Phil!"

When I was able to see Phil again, he had wires coming from everywhere and pumps on his legs to prevent blood clots. The next ten days were horrible, and many things went wrong, including blocked catheters and excruciating back pain that led to more X-rays, lung scans, and an angiogram. Phil had been scheduled to go home the next day, but it appeared that wasn't going to happen.

I didn't want to leave Phil's side, but we both realized our eight-year-old boys desperately needed their mom's positive attitude and reassurance that their dad was going to be just fine.

7/23/94

I have just left the most wonderful man, so full of Your love and grace, back in ICU! Lord we continue to praise You. We know a mighty work is being done in Phil, but does it have to be so painful? The angiogram found a large hole in Phil's heart with tons of blood clots in his lungs. With the hole in his heart and so many blood clots, he was sent back to ICU. He has oxygen again up his nose. Wires and IV tubes hooked up everywhere. Oh Lord, I don't question You, but why did you have him ready to go home and then slam him back in ICU with spasms of pain?

Phil had to stay in the ICU motionless for three days, followed by four more days in a regular bed. They checked his blood every day to ensure the clots were dissolving.

Phil was mentally in anguish. Tears streamed down his face as he cried out to me in desperation about losing his own dad at eight years of age. His treasured sons were the same age.

"Please Lord, let me see my boys grow up," he prayed through his sobs.

Phil sunk into a depression. He spent his time staring blankly at nothing. I put the word out.

Guys from church arrived and other friends flew in, all to love on this giant of a man and to pray with him. He was so grateful for all of the support, and the cloud lifted. He was so thankful for the incredible nurses who were taking care of him and for whatever time he had left with the boys and me.

Several of us left the ICU feeling like we had been blessed by Phil's humbleness, his tears, and his open emotions. With tears of joy, I thank You Jesus that I have the privilege of being married to this man.

Once Phil was released to a regular room, we realized we really needed to start praying for his recovery and a job. Through all of the health scares, we completely forgot that Phil didn't have a job.

One afternoon, we were walking the hallways. Phil was in his hospital gown, catheter in place, tubes hanging, holding onto the IV pole. He had a scruffy beard and his hair was sticking out in tufts here and there. His feet shuffled as we walked along.

The elevator doors open and three men in black suits walked past us.

We slowly shuffled back to his room. Just walking the hallway was exhausting for him. We entered his hospital room, and the three men we had passed were standing at attention with their hands crossed in front. They looked very official. One stepped forward.

"Are you Phil Mogle?" he said.

Phil nodded, and the man handed him a sealed note. They left.

We stared at each other. Who were those people?

Exhausted, Phil got back into bed and opened the note.

It was from an old Marriott friend. He was now the Vice President of Sales. He wished Phil a speedy recovery and asked him to rejoin the Marriott team whenever he felt up to it.

Who were the men who had brought the note? We never found out. Maybe they were angels!

Our emotions had been raw the entire past two weeks, but this sent us both into tears of joy, full of gratitude. For the first time in weeks, Phil prayed over our family and thanked God for His faithfulness in providing such wonderful doctors, nurses, and now – a job!

After three weeks in Rahway Hospital, Phil walked out into the sunshine. He said the air on his skin felt weird and his eyes had to adjust from looking beyond just four walls.

Dr. Murphy said Phil would have to come in every three months for an out-patient check on the inside of his bladder via a cystoscopy. Phil said this procedure always kept him in touch with his own mortality. He was beyond grateful every time the results came back clear.

Phil's long-term diagnosis was bleak, but he felt great and his health returned. I couldn't imagine life without Phil in any way. We always prayed for our boys, but we prayed even more fervently now that we'd been faced with the real possibility that they may lose their dad. We especially prayed for their tween and teenage years. We knew prayer was the mightiest weapon we had to fight for our boys to make good choices.

Our deepest desire was to spend as much time together as possible. Phil's new job required a good bit of traveling, so we decided to homeschool the boys. We loved the flexibility homeschool offered us. If Phil was going to Boston, we went with him and studied the Boston Tea Party and The Revolutionary War. When our lessons took us to Miami, we studied and visited the Everglades and ecosystems. In San Diego, we learned about early 1800s California and irrigation systems (a nod to Phil's family being in the water business), while squeezing in our USC football games – no homework required!

Between traveling with Phil, flying internationally for work, flying to LA for games, and grading papers and preparing lessons in hotel rooms or on flights while passengers slept, I was exhausted. When Phil realized I had not slept in the same time zone for more than ten days, he stepped up.

"Enough. You and the boys are staying home for a while."

Relief flooded over all of us.

When Phil was still living in New Orleans and working for Marriott, he had a very important client named Roy, the Vice President of the Professional Convention Management Association (PCMA). Roy brought a large amount of traffic and business to Marriott through a yearly meeting that drew over 2,500 people. It was Phil's job to make sure Roy never took his meeting to any other hotel.

Over the years, Roy became a dear friend – more like a brother. Phil and Roy developed a strong bond over their similar views on business and sales. Our boys called him Uncle Roy.

For years, our family jumped on one of my planes over Christmas for a trip to Birmingham, Alabama, and celebrated the holiday with Uncle Roy and his family. We loved the southern charm of Birmingham. Everything was close with no long commutes. Roy lived only five minutes from the main headquarters of PCMA. Each time we visited, we were enamored by the exceptionally convenient airport, the quality and style of the neighborhoods, the great reputation of the schools, and the friendliness of the people. At the end of our time, we hugged Roy and his daughters goodbye. Our sweet family of four was like a merry, exhausted band of traveling gypsies.

Roy always ended our visits with a wink.

"One day I'm going to steal you away from Marriott."

But Marriott had other plans for Phil.

ON THE MOVE AGAIN

For two California beach kids, New York City was captivating and just plain fun. Phil's Marriott office was smack dab in the middle of Manhattan at 42nd and Lexington. With plays and dinners – some with business clients and others just for the two of us – we were like two lovers on an adventure. Our home in Edison, New Jersey, had a touch of New England flair. Our neighbors had that wonderful New Jersey straightforwardness that is actually quite awesome; we always knew where they stood! We had a great church and were making so many good memories, but Marriott decided they needed us in Washington, D.C.

Phil was offered a promotion to take over the Southeast Region as Vice President of Marketing. We decided to make the move.

Phil had one last visit with Dr. Murphy. During this appointment, she told Phil that he just might be one of the 18% that beats this monster. She committed to send records to his new doctor in Virginia. He would need to keep up the tests, but she now recommended them only every six months for the next two years. If those went well, he could drop down to once a year. His tearful ICU prayer to see his boys grow up was becoming more real.

On October 25, 1996, the Mayflower moving crew loaded up our home and hit the road. The boys, Baba, cats, dog, and I piled into our big red van. Phil drove his car, and our little caravan headed south for our new home in Sterling, Virginia.

The Mayflower crew finished unloading all our stuff.

"See you in two years," the driver said.

"What?"

We all had quizzical looks on our faces. He laughed.

"You Marriott people move every two years," he said.

Humph, not us, I thought.

Phil worked just outside of Washington, D.C., with a fifty-minute commute. No matter what city they were in, he and Roy managed to meet up for dinner as often as they could. They loved discussing the state of the hotel convention industry and how they envisioned its future. Roy was excited that our move had brought us a little closer, about a one-hour flight from Birmingham.

This new move still didn't keep us from our beloved USC football games. A game that made the history books happened on November 30, 1996. We were there, along with 90,029 other screaming fans.

The matchup was between USC and long-time rival Notre Dame. Las Vegas oddsmakers called it an eight-million-dollar game.

It pains me to say this, but in 1996, USC was a mediocre team. Notre Dame was dominant, and they'd beaten us for thirteen years straight. It was their head coach Lou Holtz's final game.

We entered the Coliseum in our game gear full of Trojan spirit, screaming, "We're number one!" We sat on the five-yard line about forty rows up, close to the east end of the field. We were in the Notre Dame section, looking across to the USC students. Our adorable song leaders, massive marching band, and the team lined up along the field. The game began.

Phil, being the passionate Trojan he was, focused on every play of every game, and his sons followed in his footsteps.

During the first quarter, we scored two field goals, making the score 6-0. In the second quarter, Notre Dame answered with a touchdown, bringing the score to 6-7. During half time, Phil struck up a conversation with the man sitting next to us. Notre Dame scored again during the third quarter, and the score was 6-14. Phil was still so engrossed in conversation with the stranger that I don't think he even noticed the touchdown.

The fourth quarter was packed with action – we scored, then they scored, then we scored. The game was tied at 20-20 and we were going into overtime! The stadium was buzzing, and hope had risen up inside every USC fan. This could be it; we might actually break the streak! Every fan was on their feet and screaming their head off...all except for Phil and the man sitting next to us. They were bent over, and, due to the extreme noise, drawn close to each other talking. The boys kept glancing at their dad, wondering why he didn't appear to care about the game.

During overtime, USC scored and won the game 27-20. It was Lou Holtz's last game as the coach of the Irish and his first loss to the Trojans.

After the game was over, we all asked Phil what on earth had been so import-ant to cause him to miss the entire last half of the game. He explained that the man sitting next to him had attended the game with his son because the tickets had been given to them. They weren't fans of either team; they had just come for the experience.

We still didn't understand. What had been more important than the game?

Phil continued to explain that the man was going through rough times and had completely opened up to him. Phil used this opportunity to share the gospel of Jesus, and the man accepted Christ as his Lord and Savior right there, in the middle of an action-packed football game with over 90,000 screaming fans.

Not only did that man's life change for eternity, but Phil's actions that night also impacted our boys in a mighty way. As college students and businessmen, both Matt and Mark have shared this story to reach others. Phil showed his two young sons where his greatest loyalty was – not just by his words, but also by his actions.

RETIRING MY WINGS

Just like in our prior homes, our home in D.C. provided Baba with a great space on the main level. As usual, we piled into her room to watch USC football and whatever else was on TV. On August 31, 1997, we watched with the rest of the world as the BBC reported a high-speed car crash involving Princess Diana. Early reports claimed that she was injured with no further details. Soon, we all realized the truth. Baba's room was a place for great conversations – both about sports and the whys of life.

The Baltimore USAir base only had domestic flights, so I had no more treks to Paris or Frankfurt. The three-and-four-day trips were taking a toll on our family. My flight schedule wasn't working for us anymore. I didn't feel any attachment to the flight crews or my fellow flight attendants like I had with my PSA family.

After twenty-eight years of flight service, I turned in my resignation in October of 1997. USAir had undergone a huge expansion and they were up to 11,000 flight attendants. Seniority was everything in the airline industry. By the time I resigned, I was No. 338. If only I could have sold that number!

The biggest blessing that came from our move to the Washington, D.C., area was Phil's ability to be home more. The boys easily talked him into being one of the coaches for their little league team, the Yankees. They still remember their dad's advice.

"Just go have some fun."

And fun they had. They even won the Loudon County Northern Virginia Little League Championship!

Phil had completely recovered and adjusted to his life after surgery. Dr. Murphy had cautioned him that with two-thirds of his bladder removed, he would always need to stay close to restroom facilities. For him, this proved to be totally false. Phil led a completely normal life. Our prayers were being answered.

We found a new doctor in Virginia who agreed with Dr. Murphy's treatment plan, which continued as scheduled. Every six months, when his report came back clear, our hope increased that he had beaten this cancer. Any time he could be with his boys, he grabbed it. And any time we had the opportunity to sneak out after they were put to bed, we did, thanks to Baba giving us those one to two hours of freedom. Even if it was just grabbing an ice cream cone or a cold beer, we treasured our time together.

Phil adjusted to his new marketing position at Marriott. He was in charge of the entire Southeast Region. He loved working with all of his old Marriott buddies, but it was a large corporation. Everything had to go through the proper channels for any new changes or ideas. Phil's entrepreneurial concepts were futuristic, and the corporate world did not move at this pace. As a family, we continued our annual Christmas visits to Roy and his family in Birmingham.

Phil was expected to entertain often, including lots of conventions and late dinners, which I attended with him as much as possible. His commute was over fifty minutes, and he often arrived home after the boys' and my bedtimes. Over time, his travel picked up immensely.

I took the boys into D.C. often to visit the museums. We played on The Mall, the grassy area between the U.S. Capitol building and the Washington Monument, flanked by all the Smithsonian museums. We enjoyed the beauty and history of where we lived. We visited Civil War sites, and we especially loved seeing the cherry blossoms in the spring, floating down the Potomac River that ran close by our home.

Phil was speaking more and more at hotel convention events with increased travel. He was known as a leader in the industry and a man of integrity. We had always prayed over our family, but it was now common to pray over the phone at bedtime. We prayed for the boys, for our family, and for any decisions we had coming up. We always ended the same.

"Lord God, not our will but yours be done in our lives."

The months went on. Finally, after much prayer and an incredible offer, Roy prevailed.

Phil accepted the position of Chief Operating Officer with PCMA in Birmingham, Alabama. PCMA is a nonprofit foundation with thousands of members and leaders in the business community, such as the American College of Cardiology, the City of San Antonio, the Association of Railroad Engineers, etc. It is operated by a board of directors.

The last boxes were loaded into the moving company van. The final items to be packed were our Christmas ornaments, lights, and our five-foot life-size Santa decked out in his red velvet suit. The boys had a plan – before we unpacked any boxes at our new home, it would be decorated for Christmas.

On December 9, 1998, our van was loaded up with two boys, two cats, two dogs (we'd gained a dog during our time in Virginia), Baba, and me. Once again, Phil followed behind in his car, which was packed to the ceiling. Before we pulled out of the driveway, we asked for God's blessing on our drive south. We prayed that this would be our last move ever. It was time for the boys to make friends they wouldn't part with in two years. We knew that the school system in Vestavia Hills, a suburb of Birmingham, was incredible. With Phil's promotion and the lower housing costs in Alabama, we could finally start saving and investing. This move to Alabama definitely would be a profitable one.

And Phil had been cancer-free with neither pain nor symptoms for four years.

SOUTHERN ROOTS

December 1998 was as busy as they come. We got the boys registered at school, and Phil set up his new office at the PCMA headquarters. Our life-size Santa in the window quickly endeared us to the families in the neighborhood. Putting up Christmas decorations was far more important than figuring out where to put pots and pans!

True to Southern tradition, our new neighbors loved their lights and glitter with candles in every window. Spotlights shone on front doors where large, gorgeous wreaths hung, adorned in wide gold ribbons intertwined with enormous red bows. Whether in their little girls' hair or their Christmas wreaths, southerners love their bows!

After Christmas vacation ended, we established a normal routine for everyone. When in town, Phil drove the boys to school every day. Even with traffic, the school was only eight minutes away. This drive became the most treasured time of the day for all three of them. They talked about coaches, sports, and USC football. Before they got out, Phil prayed over them! The PCMA office was directly behind the school.

On their first day at Pizitz Middle School, the boys quickly realized that while they were sitting in the cafeteria, they could see their dad sitting at his desk up the hill. Later that day while I was sitting in the carpool line, I received a phone call. It was the boys, giggling hysterically, saying they were already sitting at Phil's desk. This became a daily routine – our race to Phil's office. I was beginning to think our move to Vestavia Hills was the best decision ever.

When meeting someone in the South, it's not uncommon to ask where they go to church or whether they cheer for Alabama or Auburn – or, better yet, Roll Tide or War Eagle? Church and football, all in the same breath. One of the only drawbacks of Birmingham was being a USC Trojan from the Pac-10. Living in SEC territory wasn't easy!

It was time to find a church that would work for tweens, a senior, and Phil and me. Even at school, the boys were asked what church and what youth group they attended. Several church names kept popping up, but I wanted to talk to the youth pastors and also check out what senior programs were available. Phil and I figured that if we found a church that worked for both Baba and the boys, it would also work for us.

About eight weeks into our new life in the South, we agreed on Shades Mountain Baptist Church. We all found our niche and settled in. The boys absolutely loved their youth group and youth pastor, an incredible young guy who related to the boys and their friends. Pastor Jay always listened and took their concerns seriously, never minimizing their feelings. This was the height of the What Would Jesus Do movement, and Pastor Jay had a way of bringing in God's word and making the students think about how Jesus would handle social, school, and relationship pressures.

We loved their school, teachers, and coaches. Vestavia Hills was a close-knit community, so it took some time to get acquainted and fit in. Everybody already knew everybody. However, having two cute athletic boys helped tremendously. Soon, the response to our introduction was, "Oh, you're Matt and Mark's parents." We began to run into their teachers at the grocery store, and some doubled as our Sunday School teachers. We had moved so many times before, but this felt different. It began to feel like this was home for good.

Unlike Phil or me, the boys grew up with Jesus in their lives, surrounded by our family talks and prayers. We always told them that when they felt ready, they could get baptized. We wanted them to fully understand what Jesus dying on the cross meant for them, for their eternity.

In the late '90s, a youth program was traveling around the country called *Heaven's Gates and Hell's Flames*. The program came to our church. It was introduced by muscle men who broke bricks with their bare hands, biceps bursting out of their sleeves – the perfect thing to grab the attention of middle-school-aged boys! These muscle men talked about their changed lives, how Jesus Christ had given them the hope and strength they needed to turn away from their past addictions. They introduced the theatrical part of the program.

For the next forty-five minutes, actors played out terrible situations full of divorce, unwanted pregnancies, failure in school, drinking, and drugs. The next scene showed Satan and his demons gleefully pulling the strings to make these people miserable, even to the point of contemplating suicide. The whole time, angels stood in the background, silent against the wall. In the next act, a friend, relative, or teacher came in and suggested they pray together. This awakened the angels, and the battle began. The drama on stage showed how prayer works and how God goes to battle for us, not wanting to lose any of us.

After the play was over, Pastor Danny prayed and asked if anyone wanted to claim Jesus as their Lord and Savior. Many got up out of their seats and walked up to the stage, including our two boys and one of Roy's daughters. We returned again the next night. This time, Baba wanted to go forward to rededicate her life to Christ. Mark walked up front with her.

The next Sunday, April 18, 1999, our boys and forty other people were all baptized. With eyes full of tears, Phil and I were beyond happy. Phil always said, "Just be there!" We knew that meant to be in heaven. It was quite the celebration!

Two days later, the world changed again.

At 11:19 a.m. on April 20, 1999, Eric Harris and Dylan Klebold began shooting on the campus of Columbine High School in Littleton, Colorado. By 12:08 p.m., gunfire had ceased. Twelve students, one teacher, and the two shooters were dead. Many more were injured as they tried to escape the school. At that time, it was the worst school shooting in U.S. history.

We all watched the news in absolute horror, not comprehending the violence or hatred that led to this. Just like the airplane crashes or the cancer phone call from Dr. Murphy, life can change or end in the twinkling of an eye.

Where will you spend eternity?

ONE CHANGE TO ANOTHER

In November 1999, we were coming up on one year in Vestavia Hills. The entire family loved it. Phil and I regularly walked the dogs through the neighborhood.

One night on our walk, we were at the top of a hill, headed for home. Phil had been unusually quiet the entire time. Finally, he took a deep breath followed by a heavy sigh.

"The board has decided to move PCMA to Chicago."

I sat down in the middle of the street and cried.

"We can't do it. We can't move the boys again," I said.

Phil completely agreed. The boys had adjusted so well and had fabulous friends, as did we. We loved everything about where we were. We decided against the move, and this decision led us down yet another path. Phil and Roy decided it was a great time to start their own consulting business.

Phil spent the next year getting PCMA ready for its move to Chicago. The company's last day in Birmingham was October 31, 2000. On the same day, Phil and Roy officially began their consulting business.

Both men were exceptionally connected and highly respected. Their expertise would be in high demand. No one doubted that Phil and Roy would become extremely successful on their own. Their business would mostly be conducted either by phone or elsewhere around the country, and the Birmingham airport made it super easy for commuting.

As the dawn of a new millennium approached, the world buzzed with panic and anticipation. I stocked up on a ton of gallon water jugs, but Y2K came and went. Nothing happened.

Anyone starting a business knows they may have to tap into their own money reserves. We had no problem doing this. We didn't have one ounce of concern over the future success of Phil and Roy's business. Once we went through our savings, we were able to take hardship loans from our retirement accounts. We knew full well that we would repay ourselves and avoid the hefty fines. This, too, was not an issue for either of us.

Phil could not have been happier. He was home more than he could ever remember, always able to be with his boys. He went to their baseball and football practices. Our new home had a jacuzzi out on the deck, and it became the family conversation pit. We often sat and just listened as the boys talked, vented, and laughed. What more could parents of teenagers ask for?

SUCCESS FOR THE FATHERLESS

Losing his dad at the age of eight was extremely difficult for Phil. Not only did Phil miss his dad terribly, but he felt there were so many things that only a dad can pass on to his son.

It was now early 2001. Phil's cancer was something we rarely talked or even thought about, except when he had his cystoscope check-ups. Still, Phil wanted people to know – wanted his boys to know – that it was possible for them to be successful without him, their father.

We prayed this would never happen, but between consulting contracts, Phil began to write a book entitled *Success for the Fatherless*.

Here is an excerpt from the book:

The process of being a father has also allowed me to understand what I missed and the impact of this void on my life. Fathers are an irreplaceable part of a child's life. From personal experience I can attest that success can still be attained and much of what was missed can be overcome, but to be honest, it will never be as good as having a dad...

As a "guy" and the youngest in my family, I could never imagine changing a baby's diaper. It was beyond me how anyone could babysit a baby or a toddler and I promised myself that changing a diaper was something I would never do.

This was before I had my twin sons. Even while my wife was pregnant I still could not imagine myself changing a diaper. That all changed in the delivery room when they placed my twin sons in my arms immediately following their births. I carried them for the first two hours of their lives as they were measured, weighed, and checked out. I found a passion that March 20th in 1986 that I had never known before. I became a father!

These beautiful (to me anyway) little babies were mine and for the first time in my life I truly understood that there is something that you will give your life for. This was something! My sons instantaneously instilled in me a feeling I had not known before or expected. I can say that changing diapers became the most natural (still not enjoyable) thing in the world along with all sorts of new things I never imagined I could do.

HOW MUCH MORE?

Phil worked from home, and our dining room table became his office. It wasn't exactly a private work environment, but he loved it. The boys knew that their dad was always available for them unless he was on a call or dictating into his microphone. Since he was at home, Phil also was able to share in more chores around the house.

We lived on a corner lot in a heavily wooded neighborhood. This required gutter and leaf clean-up several times a year, especially leading into fall. While working one day, Phil had a small slip on the roof and then another off a short ladder in the yard. Both times, he landed on his right side. He noticed that his hip began to ache. It progressed to the point where it was painful to walk. He figured he had bruised his bone or tweaked his back.

We always walked the dogs in the evening together, but one night shortly following the falls, he was in too much pain.

"Honey, I can't go. You walk the dogs by yourself."

Phil was strong and healthy, and I didn't have much patience.

"Time to find a doctor, buddy," I teased. "You probably need some physical therapy!"

Phil's urologist thought it was a back problem – maybe a slipped disk – and sent him to a neurosurgeon. They found nothing. They sent him to a physical therapist to work out the pain. It got worse and became so intense that they began to think he had cracked his pelvis. He was sent to a hip specialist at HealthSouth.

During his appointment with this new doctor, Phil described his last seven years of medical history. The doctor ordered a complete bone scan. With Phil's cancer gone, we thought at the most he'd need a hip replacement. We truly thought it would be an easy fix.

Nothing prepared us for what came next. After a few days, we went back to the doctor and reviewed the scan.

A softball-sized tumor had attached itself to Phil's pelvis. Several other "hot spots" had shown up on Phil's body scan. HealthSouth sent us to the oncology department at the University of Alabama at Birmingham (UAB), an internationally known teaching hospital. Fortunately, many of our dear friends from church practiced medicine there, including two of Phil's best friends, Dr. Peter and Dr. Richard.

MRIs, CT scans, and X-rays were quickly scheduled. Phil also needed a bone biopsy, which required an overnight stay. The oncologist, Dr. R, said that once we had all the results, we could easily start a plan of action. He sounded upbeat and confident.

The bone biopsy was scheduled for the next Tuesday. Phil and I were at complete peace. We just knew that God would use our story and that Phil would be – already was – healed.

Tuesday rolled around, and it was a beautiful blue-sky morning. Before we drove to UAB, I had time to walk the dogs. As I rounded the corner to head back home, I noticed two construction workers in the back of their truck, intently watching a small TV. They seemed mesmerized, worry written all over their faces. My curiosity took over. I walked over and asked what they were watching. They stepped back and pointed to the screen.

"A plane just crashed into the World Trade Center."

It was September 11, 2001.

I hurried home and walked in the door. Phil and Baba already had the TV on; the second plane had hit the second tower. We got in the car and headed downtown for our appointment.

I dropped Phil off at the front of the building while I parked the car. UAB is a huge hospital complex with many buildings and bridges to connect them. By the time I arrived in the outpatient surgery center, Phil was already in a hospital gown, once again watching the mayhem in New York City. We stood in silent horror. To this day, most Americans know exactly where they were on that fateful day. At the mention of September 11, people grow quiet, like they are grieving all over again. Our grieving had just begun.

After the biopsy, it took ten days for Dr. R to get all the results back. Once again, we sat across from him in his office to get the results. This time, he did not look confident.

He spoke slowly, almost as if he were apologizing, regretting the words that were coming out of his mouth.

"The cancer you had seven years ago never left your body. It was just lying dormant. It's as if your falls awoke a sleeping giant that had been hiding. The cancer is everywhere. The largest tumor has attached itself to your pelvic bone, but it is intertwined into everything – all your organs. It is inoperable. I'm so sorry."

He went on to say chemo may or may not shrink it. Chemo would not cure it, but it may make Phil more comfortable. Phil held my hand and we drove home in silence.

After our kick-in-the-gut diagnosis, we had a football game.

9/20/01

God is so good in the way He comforts us – we had a special treat at the 9th grade football game. Matt made the first high school pass to Mark, 35 yards – a Mogle to a Mogle! It was so awesome, Lord. We needed that. Thank you, God.

That night, we put the boys to bed like normal. We kneeled down, sang our two songs, said our prayers, and kissed them good night. Phil and I had not yet digested his horrible health news; we couldn't tell the boys. Not yet, anyway. Before going to sleep ourselves, we prayed for guidance, wisdom, and healing. We held each other until we fell asleep.

Phil's first six-hour round of chemo would be in two weeks. That gave us plenty of time to talk with the boys. We were having a normal jacuzzi night with all of us sitting together. The boys were laughing, telling stories, and being silly, and Phil and I just listened. Finally, Phil interrupted them and said we had something we needed to talk about.

We told them how the cancer had returned, how it had stayed hidden and silently grown everywhere. They had a few questions, and we ended in prayer asking God to take this cancer from our family. We all went to bed that night in denial. We were just going through the motions. We truly believed God would heal Phil – their dad, my beloved husband.

10/26/01

We are here at UAB for our second 6-hour round of chemo. We are far more prepared and aware of how Phil's body will handle this. Phil is blown away by the outpouring of love, prayers, and FOOD. Our next-door neighbors, Alan and Darryl, have made it their personal mission to make sure our front yard stays in tip-top condition. They have their own huge yards, but they worked for hours to make ours look perfectly groomed. Phil, near tears, said they aren't just running a lawnmower around – they are giving us their best efforts! He feels terrible; he is so wiped out. Lord, we continue to place ourselves at your feet. We trust you with the cancer, our provision, the business. We are beginning to wonder what we should be doing on top of the treatments...sell, rent, move? Lord, if we are out of Your will, PUSH us to where You want us. Not our will but YOURS.

11/9/01

Dear Lord, we are here at UAB, ha! You know where we are, but it comforts me so to talk with You! Phil's white blood count, platelets, and red blood count are all out of whack so no treatment today. This is what is making Phil feel so weak, exhausted, and out-of-breath. He also has what appears to be a blood clot in his right calf. Go figure – how does one get a blood clot when counts are so low? We are waiting to see what they want us to do.

Roy and Phil continued to build their consulting business, but with Phil laid up, it was getting increasingly more difficult. Roy was running double duty and getting ragged.

In mid-November, Dr. R asked Phil about his pain, and Phil reported that he didn't have any; he was just tired. Dr. R was confused. The tumor had not shrunk one bit. The terrible pain Phil had back in August should still be there, but it wasn't. Dr. R ordered another bone scan.

Had the tumor died from the inside out? Radiation was scheduled to start the next week. Dr. R explained that the laser beam could pinpoint the (hopefully) now dead tumor and dissolve it. Our hearts raced with hope. Not only did Phil want to get back to work, but we desperately needed the income.

Late December was hard. The tumor hadn't died. Phil's pain came back, and the radiation didn't seem to be dissolving anything. Work slowed down. Matt and Mark didn't ask for anything for Christmas.

12/27/01

Lord, we prayed to You for our financial needs, and we have been blessed beyond anything we imagined! We have been blessed by those in our church family. Phil's mom and sister have totally carried us for November and December. My brother has also helped. Others have come by to give us checks saying that we had blessed them in the past and now they wanted to do the same for us. Oh Lord, I pray for the day we can share once again with those in need! Father, the treatments don't seem to be doing anything for Phil. We've both talked about how the doctors one day will finally say, "That's it, there is nothing more we can do." And that is when You will step in and miraculously cure Phil. Lord, I know You can operate in any way You choose, and I pray that no matter what, Phil, the boys, and I will praise Your Holy Name.

SWEET 16

We eased into 2002. Phil continued his treatments. He actually began feeling really well, and his spirits were high. Dr. R said the tumor had shrunk 35%.

When PCMA left Alabama, we went on COBRA and had to start paying for our own medical insurance. The premiums were $1,000.00 a month along with a huge yearly deductible that started all over again on January 1. Between our insurance, mortgage, utilities, food, and everything else, money was beyond tight.

The boys' sixteenth birthday was coming up. In the school parking lot at Vestavia Hills, it was common to see BMWs, Hummers, Honda Accords, and Jeep Wranglers; getting a car for a sixteenth birthday was a big deal. Mark had always talked about how he wanted to drive a Ford F-150. Matt wanted a Jeep Grand Cherokee. We dreaded telling them that not only were they not getting their dream cars, but they'd also have to share the big red Dodge Ram van with Mom.

During one of our jacuzzi nights, Phil and I broke the news to the boys.

They weren't surprised or disappointed. We asked them what we could get them for their big day instead. Both boys said they wanted a super nice leather-bound Bible.

What? Two sixteen-year-old boys only wanted a Bible? What an immense blessing they were to us.

In my experience, the wife is usually the gift-buyer and the husband just signs the card when it's put in front of him. This is a generalization, of course, but some might be able to relate. However, for this birthday, this wasn't the case. Phil was the one who wanted to go to Lifeway Christian Bookstore and pick out the Bibles for the boys. When it came time to wrap them, I was planning to write something on the inside and just have him sign *Love, Dad*. But Phil said he wanted to do the writing. I broke into tears as I read what he wrote to each of our young men.

Everything I am as a man, husband, and father,

I have learned from this Book.
I love you, Dad

We also took the boys to a Steven Curtis Chapman concert. At the concert, a special guest appeared by the name of Steve Saint. Steve was the son of Nate Saint, a missionary in Ecuador. In 1956, Nate, along with four other fellow missionaries, was speared to death by a native tribe in the jungle.

Steve came out on stage and spoke. He then introduced a man named Mincaye and brought him out on the stage.

Mincaye was the very person who had speared Steve's father to death. Afterward, God transformed Mincaye's life, and Steve was able to forgive him. The two men now dearly loved each other; Steve's own family called Mincaye "Grandfather." They now traveled the world together, telling about God's mercy and forgiveness. Only God could write a story like that! Over the years, Steve and Mincaye's powerful story reached thousands and thousands of people. We sat in awe as we listened to Steve say that God never wastes a hurt, and he can transform any life if we let him.

Our drive home from the concert was full of conversation about Mincaye. How could Steve possibly forgive him? And now Mincaye was part of Steve's family! We connected this with the impossible nature of God's forgiveness toward us. What a way to launch into our sons' sixteenth birthday!

STUDYING PROVERBS

In March and April, Phil devoured history books. Over a two-week period, he underlined and made comments in all 631 pages of *The Timetables of History*. He read entire books – not just chapters – in the Bible. He was in awe of how the entire Bible told the story of Jesus, from the first page to the last. He zeroed in on Proverbs, realizing it was a study on life and how to handle any situation. He told me that he wanted to go over this book with the boys. He was so excited at the thought of sitting down and studying with them.

"Hey, Proverbs talks about sex, adultery, marriage, money, working, business ethics…what better stuff to go over with my guys?"

For the entire month of April, the boys hurried home from school to be with their dad and study a chapter a day out of Proverbs. I never heard one word they said to each other; the conversations remained completely between the guys. To this day, both boys treasure this time they spent with him and the conversations they had. Phil didn't make excuses or push it off until later. We weren't sure if later would ever come.

Phil became more tired, and it became more and more difficult for him to find a comfortable place to sit. He was only able to sit in the recliner or lie on his left side on the couch.

Around mid-May, he put aside his writing on *Success for the Fatherless*, just for now. It was already up to 180 pages. There was just a bit more to finish, and he said he'd do it next month.

THE BEST AND WORST OF TIMES

5/24/02

This past week Phil has been very sleepy. His walking has become like a shuffle, his conversation slower. We all attribute this to the radiation.

Phil had a Friday morning routine of meeting with his friend Dr. Richard at Edgar's Bakery to eat and pray for their sons. They'd been doing this for years. On this Friday morning in late May, he met Dr. Richard like usual. He returned home from Edgar's around 8:30 a.m. and fell asleep in his recliner.

He had a luncheon business appointment at 11:00, so I woke him up around 10:00. Immediately, I noticed something was terribly wrong.

Within ten minutes, I had him in the car. We rushed toward UAB's ER. Looking back, I realize I should've called 911.

Phil was slurring his words and repeating himself.

"I'm OK. I have an appointment I have to get to."

I assured him this would only take just a minute, but we needed to go to UAB.

I pulled into the circular drive in front of the ER and ran in.

"My husband is having a stroke!" I yelled.

Within seconds, they had him out of the car and lying down on a gurney. They rushed him inside, and I hurried to find a parking space.

I circled up the spiral parking garage ramp with tears streaming down my face, praying.

Lord I have no clue why this is happening, but this has got to be for your glory.

I found a space on the fifth floor. I figured that taking the stairs would be faster than waiting on the elevator, so I rushed into the stairwell. The ER was several buildings and blocks away. As I ran down the stairs, a man was running up. It just happened to be our good friend Dr. Peter. Between sobs, I quickly blurted out what had happened.

He turned on his heels and sprinted back down the stairs.

"Follow me!" he shouted back over his shoulder.

Over the next five minutes, we weaved in and out of doorways, hallways, and bridges that connected buildings. We entered the final employees-only stairwell, and it opened up into the back section of the ER. Within seconds, we were next to Phil's bedside.

Dr. Peter normally parked in the doctor's garage, but he hadn't that morning; he later told me that he never parks in that garage. He was in the stairwell at the exact moment we bumped into each other. I know God was watching over Phil and me.

By 4:00 p.m., Phil had been moved to the Neuro ICU (NICU). The doctors had discovered that Phil's blood had gotten so thin that a large pool had formed in his brain. At 3:00 a.m., Phil went into a coma. The doctors needed to put a vent in his skull to keep pressure down and drain off the blood. Even in his coma, he went through withdrawals from the pain medication he'd been on.

The next few days were pure hell.

Word got out and prayers went up. I left the hospital only to go home and sleep. Women from church came into our home and cleaned it from top to bottom. They washed clothes and changed sheets. They had it all organized – a cleaning crew, a cooking crew, a crew to care for the boys, and a phone line for prayers and information. These women were *so* thoughtful. They even had a rotation of people come in and sit with Baba, just to talk and be with her while her son was in the hospital. I felt God's presence with us everywhere!

Lord, this has to be for your glory, I kept praying, all the while also praying for God to heal my cherished husband.

I really don't remember much over the next few days other than being in the waiting room and only being allowed into the NICU for a brief fifteen minutes every four hours. It's funny how complete strangers go from staring blankly at the waiting room walls to immediately bonding, speaking lovingly about their relatives lying in beds just beyond the closed doors. We all staked out our spots and hunkered down in the not-so-comfortable chairs. We got to know each other by sharing stories of how and why our loved ones were there. Some had been behind those doors for months. Family members brought in blankets and pillows. We made this thirty-foot square room home.

It was so hard for the boys to see their dad this sick. In their eyes, he was a giant of a man. Now, he couldn't even open his eyes. We knew Phil could hear us because he calmed down when the boys held his hands. We sensed that he knew his guys were there. By Sunday, he had still not opened his eyes but was able to move his head for a yes or no. He even squeezed the boys' hands and held up his fist for a high five. The nurses kept telling us how amazed they were by how well he was doing.

5/26/02

If somehow, through all this, people can see that our peace, our calm, our faith, our trust, and our hope reside in YOU and they want to know how to have this personal relationship, then all we are going through is worth it!

The next morning, the doctor was in shock when he entered the NICU. Phil's restraints, which had been placed for his safety, were off, and Phil was sitting up in bed brushing his teeth. The nurses had given him a shave. To me, he looked beautiful!

Many people have heard stories of others who have died, seen heaven, and then come back to tell about it. Without a doubt, I think Phil visited heaven during his coma, perhaps even sat at the feet of Jesus.

The next ten days after Phil woke up were absolutely incredible. They were full of challenges but also truly amazing. None of us knew what Phil's recovery would look like or what the extent of the damage would be. It appeared that rehab was going to be extensive. We didn't know if he could walk, read, or what he could remember. He vacillated between a child-like awareness and adult consciousness, going from baby talk to profound prayers. One moment, it was as if he was completely healthy again. The next, he would lapse back into nothingness, as if the light plug had been pulled out of the wall. One minute, he'd be focused on a red sweater and saying over and over, "Pretty red, pretty red." The next minute, he was completely coherent and telling his friend Dr. Richard that he had prayed for his son and the band he wanted to start up.

He prayed for everyone who came around him and became known for that. Visitors came in to pray for him, and he ended up praying for them instead.

"If you want to be prayed for, go see Phil, the man in bed seven!"

All the things that were hanging over our heads before the coma were still there, and medical bills were piling up. Should we sell or rent the house? I desperately needed to get a job.

Phil and our family became endeared to the ICU nurses, as did they to us. Nurses were our lifeline, and we could tell how deeply they cared for their patients. This wasn't just a job to them. One day, a nurse came in and asked Phil if he had seen Goose and the boys.

For years, Phil's nickname for me had been "Goose." He got it from the story called Rikki-Tikki-Tavi by Rudyard Kipling. The story follows an insatiably curious mongoose on his adventures in India. I am much like that mongoose, which eventually got shortened to Goose.

Phil's response brought the nurse joy.

"Goose, Goose yes! Yes boys, boys yes!"

Another day, Phil's friend Dr. Peter came in to check on Phil. With childlike delight, Phil burst out talking.

"Peter, I love you! I love you, Peter!"

The nurses always hugged us and said they could see the love our family shared. Even in the worst of circumstances, God's light was shining through Phil.

Phil's fifty-third birthday came and went while he was in the NICU. When I returned home from the hospital each night, the boys and Baba were still up waiting for me, wanting an update. The boys now had their driver's licenses, so they brought Baba by the hospital for a bit each day. I could see on her face how heartbreaking this was for her. She tried so hard to be upbeat and positive. Roy came by all the time to visit, too. Sadly, his mom passed away during this time frame. I was completely oblivious and missed her funeral.

Later that week, he said, "I just buried my mom. I don't want to bury my best friend."

I put myself in a protective bubble mentally. Even after Roy's comment, I never thought Phil would die. Surely, God was going to heal him.

Phil continued to improve and then have setbacks. After sixteen days in the ICU, the insurance company said Phil's time was up. He would have to be moved to a normal room. I argued profusely that he did not need to be placed on the oncology floor; he needed to be where they could monitor his brain. He'd not yet gotten out of bed. No one knew if he could even stand, let alone take a step.

Before leaving the ICU, Phil had to prove that he could make it to the bathroom. I watched as the ICU nurses, with absolute love and tenderness, helped Phil up and so slowly – inch by inch – shuffled him toward the bathroom. Once he made it, he grinned like he'd just made the winning touchdown against Notre Dame.

On June 8, I hugged my NICU waiting room friends goodbye. Phil was wheeled down to the oncology floor and set up in the room directly across from the nurses' station.

GOD GAVE US A MIRACLE

The following Saturday night, the boys came on their own to visit their dad. Since arriving on the oncology floor, Phil had been extremely quiet. When the boys arrived, he had just returned from a trip to the bathroom and was settled back in bed, exhausted.

The nurse stood in the corner as the boys walked in.

"Hey guys, what's up?"

For the next forty-five minutes, Phil was his old self. He remembered the last high school baseball game he attended; Matt had been on third base and had stolen for home. He remembered that he missed his birthday and wanted to have a cake the next day in the hospital to celebrate. He even wanted to know how they did on their Spanish final. They talked and laughed as if nothing had happened – no stroke, no coma, no withdrawals, no cancer. Phil was 100% the dad they always knew.

The nurse left but kept coming back into the room. I think she didn't want to miss the miracle that was happening right before her eyes.

Eventually, Phil grew tired and told the guys how much he loved them. They all hugged, and the boys got up to leave.

"Bye, Dad. We love you and we'll see you tomorrow."

Excitedly, I walked with the boys to the elevator. We were all absolutely giddy. The boys couldn't stop talking about how great their dad was doing. I didn't want to leave Phil alone for his first night in a regular room, so I had decided to spend the night at the hospital. I hugged the boys at the elevator and said goodnight. They planned to bring Baba to the hospital the next day after they went to church.

As I walked back to Phil's room, I heard singing coming down the hallway. All the nurses at the station looked quizzical and walked into his room with me.

"My life is in you, Lord! My strength is in you, Lord! My hope is in you Lord! It's you, it's you!"

Phil kept singing this over and over. He held his hand out to me, indicating he wanted me to sit on the bed with him and join him in his rejoicing. He held my hand tightly, like he didn't want the moment to end while we sang.

Eventually, he slowed down and finally sank back on his pillow, saying he was tired and wanted to rest. I left the room with the nurses, and the three of us literally grabbed each other, squealing and giggling like schoolgirls.

From what they knew and read on his medical chart, what we had just witnessed truly was a miracle.

IN A TWINKLING OF AN EYE

Early Sunday morning, Phil started moving. He was tossing and turning, moaning that his head hurt. By 10:00 a.m., he was back in the NICU, wired and hooked back up.

The pool of blood in his brain had returned and was creating intense pressure inside his head. I held his hand, remembering the sweet time of singing we'd had the night before. His eyes were closed, and he'd fallen into a painful sleep. The nurses needed to stabilize Phil. They asked me to step back out to the waiting room and said they'd come get me in a few hours.

I was back with my waiting room friends, and they all asked why I had returned. I explained all that had happened, especially emphasizing the wonderful time the boys had gotten with Phil. They listened and nodded along as I talked, some with sad faces, realizing they would never have that opportunity with their loved one.

Just as I settled into my familiar chair at 11:10 a.m., the alarms went off; code blue went out over the loudspeakers, and doctors went flying into the ICU. The air in the waiting room was thick and silent. We all held our breath, wondering which loved one had set off the alarm.

I never knew I could hold my breath for thirty-nine minutes.

Finally, two nurses appeared in the waiting room doorway; their eyes met mine.

They said Phil just stopped breathing. The CPR team tried for thirty-nine minutes. It was 11:49 a.m.

About an hour later, the boys, Baba, and Roy showed up at the hospital to say goodbye to their dad, son, and best friend. We all arrived back home around 3:30 p.m. Our back deck and porch were full of the boys' entire youth group from church, and the house was packed with dear, precious friends. The pool table was covered with a huge tablecloth and more food than I can even describe. I don't know how any of this happened. The outpouring of love, support, hugs, tears, food, and friends staying with us through the night didn't stop for weeks.

Since Roy's mom had passed away the week before, he was ready to step in, plan everything, and notify everyone. I am so grateful; I was incapable. I don't know what I would have done without him. Phil's sisters flew in, one from Los Angeles and one from Hong Kong, along with my brother. Business associates that had become dear friends also came in from all over the country. Shades Mountain is a big church and the sanctuary looked full for Phil's ceremony. The line of cars going to the cemetery was more than the eye could see. This brought some sort of comfort to the boys and Baba – seeing how loved their dad and son had been.

I was in a daze. I felt like I was being led around in a fog, in a state of confused disbelief. We all were.

One week later, I received the most amazing letter from one of the NICU nurses that had taken such sweet care of Phil. It still brings tears to my eyes to know how Phil impacted the incredible nurses on this floor.

I've blocked the nurses' names for privacy.

June 14, 2002

Dear Mrs. Mogle,

I am writing this with partial reluctancy because I was planning on originally being able to write to you about what a miraculous recovery Phil made with his intraventricular hemorrhage, but now it is becoming a letter to tell you how much my heart goes out to you and your family with the news of this horrible tragedy. Phil touched mine and every other nurse who ever got the pleasure of caring for him. In fact, one of the nurses on our unit called me crying the night of Phil's death.

While Phil was on our unit I didn't have the courage to tell you how horribly sick the interventricular hemorrhage can make a person - in fact it usually kills someone when it's the size of the one that Phil had. I knew when we extubated him less than 48 hours after admission that he had more to do with his life, but I also knew that he had a long battle with cancer ahead of him. I started praying for you and Mark and Matt immediately because I know that bone cancer is a horrible debilitating disease. I called you as soon as we extubated him because, in truth, I didn't think he would "fly" off the ventilator (because it was so soon after admission). Now I know it was the Lord allowing me to give you a moment of solitude during what would become Phil's last days.

I don't know if this will bring you any comfort (how could it when we've lost such a wonderful man), but I saw Phil Friday when I was leaving work. I went into his room and asked him if he knew me and he said, "yes, yes, yes, M---, M---, M---." I laughed and asked him if B--- was taking good care of him and he said, "excellent, excellent, excellent." Then I asked where goose and the boys were and he replied, "goose and the boys, goose and the boys." He pointed at me and raised his voice and said again, "goose and the boys M---!" I guess I'm telling you this to let you know that he loved you so very much (I know you know that) and that even when the Lord was close to calling him home that he was thinking of you and the boys and the unrelenting love you all shared. I only hope that my final thoughts will be of such a love.

I admire and respect your strength and courage during Phil's final days and I wanted you to know that I will never forget the way you looked at Phil and the way the boys high fived him. I wanted you to know that I derived great pleasure from making sure you talked to him as soon as he was extubated and that I hope in my final days God will grace me with a family as strong and as warm as your own.

Please know that I don't want to upset you in this awful time, I wanted you to know that you're in my thoughts and prayers and that Phil received the most wonderful gift God can give - a loving family, a strong spirit, and a faith that was unfaltering. I know right now you may only see one set of footprints, but I know that you realize that means God is carrying you through this.

With deepest regards and warmest prayers,

M---, Registered Nurse

Neuro Intensive Care Unit

University of Alabama Birmingham

I wrote in my journal a week later.

6/21/02

It was as if You reached down and said, "No more my child – it is time for you to come Home." I know, technically, they said 11:49, but I know it was about 11:10 that Phil was already at the feet of Jesus. He was seeing first-hand what we can only imagine. Phil always said with his big smile, "All of your questions will be answered in a second."

Phil is hearing praise music; he is walking the streets of gold. Does he see us? Is he experiencing incredible joy? What was it like when he first saw Jesus? It seems each day reveals tears, sobbing and disbelief, and, yet, there is joy in knowing Phil is with You and knowing he didn't have to suffer any longer. We were praying for a miracle – all of us had been through so much. We just KNEW that You would cure Phil and we could give You all the glory. Well, You did. Sometimes our prayers are answered not like we want them and on the other side of Heaven – Phil is cured! To give You the glory though his death isn't anything I could have ever imagined, BUT that is precisely what You call us to do, isn't it?

NUMB WITH GRIEF

How does a person describe grief?

Phil's death left the biggest void imaginable.

For the first six months after, I think we all walked around in a stupor. My arms longed to wrap around him; my body ached from not being able to throw my leg over his as we cuddled before falling asleep. For brief moments, I thought suicide was the answer. I'd be with Phil; that's where I wanted to be anyway. He is in heaven, where there is no more pain, no more tears. The ache, the longing, and the loneliness was incomprehensible.

Fortunately, between the boys returning to school, their workouts for sports, their homework, and all the meals that needed to be planned, we had somewhat of a schedule. The consistency was helpful for me to stay focused.

People give various advice about how to overcome grief – clear out your spouse's closet, remove your wedding ring, start dating in the first two years. Some of those things probably work for some people, but I didn't do any of them. I've learned that each person has to deal with his or her own grief in their own way and time.

Eventually, the pain does lessen, and the memories get stronger. Laughter returns. But you never forget them or stop loving them. Out of nowhere, the smallest, most unexpected thing can bring you to sobbing tears.

GOD PROVIDES

I've heard it said that when a big life event occurs, like a death, it isn't wise to make drastic changes for a year. We didn't have a choice. Everything had to change.

Phil passed away in June of 2002. The boys were sixteen years old. Eight years prior, Phil had lost his $500,000 life insurance policy due to his first round of cancer in New Jersey (insurance laws have since changed, thank goodness). After Phil died, we were deep in debt with new medical bills. I hadn't worked since I'd retired from flying four years prior. I desperately needed to find a job. The boys and I knew we had to put our house on the market. Baba, whom the boys adored as much as ever, had to leave us after sixteen years and move back to California to live with Phil's sister. A deeply loved cat and dog had also just passed away. It could not have been a worse time for us. Honestly, if it had not been for our church and the surrounding families supporting us for months with money and food, we would've lost everything.

Due to the eight years between cancer rounds, Phil had been declared cancer-free. Because of this, he had been able to get a tiny $90,000 life insurance policy prior to his death.

About a month after Phil died, I visited my dear friend Allison's lake house. Early one morning, I was walking on a dirt road around Smith Lake, praying.

For the last month, I had heavily debated on tithing on the $90,000 I was going to get from life insurance. I desperately needed every dime and more. Surely God didn't want me to tithe on this. Normally, God does not audibly speak to me. However, as I was praying, I heard from God loud and clear through a scripture – Malachi 3:10.

8/3/02

Father, I am so very thankful for your guidance. I had been debating whether I should tithe on the insurance money. Malachi 3:10 came to me LOUD AND CLEAR – "Bring the whole tithe into the storehouse…test me now in this…if I will not open for you the windows of heaven and pour out for you a blessing until it overflows."

Initially, I argued that I didn't have a job, but I continually felt God asking me to test him. Finally, I committed to obey.

Prior to this prayer, I had not been studying Malachi. I hadn't even been reading in the Old Testament! But the direction from God was as loud and clear as an audible voice.

I did tithe on the money, and I have never looked back. To this day, tithing is a part of my life. God isn't a genie in a bottle who gives us what we want when we make offerings to Him . However, he has never forsaken us – ever! It's the joy of my heart to obey Him as a response to his goodness to me.

I needed to find a job with medical insurance, immediately. My lack of college education and a mere twenty-eight years' experience as a flight attendant got me nowhere. My options were limited. I didn't want to work nights; I needed to be home with the boys. Again, I prayed.

Lord, I will take the first job with benefits that comes my way, so shut any door where I'm not supposed to go.

I sent out applications and got some interviews at various places – a dry cleaner, a laundromat, an auto parts store, the post office, and many other retailers. They were all perfectly nice interviews. The interviewers said everything looked great and they'd call me back. After eleven interviews, no one called me back.

I continued to pray.

Lord, help me!

Due to the huge medical expenses, our previous business ventures, and real estate moves that never paid off, I was left in a completely dire financial position. I was worried and scared. I had boys to feed. We had to sell our home as soon as possible and then move, but to where? We talked about moving back to San Diego so I could return to the airlines, but moving costs money and we had none. The boys assured me of how much they loved Birmingham. They had a fantastic group of friends from their church youth group, and they loved their school. Birmingham was home, and their dad was also there.

I was feeling completely desperate.

Right after Labor Day, I got a phone call.

On the other side of the line, it was Blue Cross Blue Shield. They said they had my resume and it looked fabulous. They asked if I'd like to work for them.

To this day, I've never known how they got my resume.

The house sold by word of mouth; we didn't even have to put up a sign. I got more cash out of it than expected, and we were able to get a cute two-bedroom garden home in the same school district. The entire Vestavia Hills football team pitched in on a Saturday and had us moved in by noon.

This comfortable, cozy home was always full of the boys' friends. Our home became known among the parents for being a safe place for any kid at any time.

For the next four years, Blue Cross Blue Shield became my home and provided a wonderful stepping stone for a fabulous job at The Ōnin Group for the following fourteen years. At Ōnin, I was in challenged to bring corporate consistency to the company, and I began to develop the skeleton framework for the future Human Resources Department. My customer service skills were put to work. I gained a reputation for being able to handle any complaint call. If a call came in, send them to Sandee!

Over the years, Proverbs 30:8 has kept me right where I need to be. It reads, "Give me neither poverty nor riches; feed me with the food that is my portion, that I not be full and deny you and say, 'Who is the LORD?' Or that I not be in want and steal, and profane the name of my God."

I am so thankful that God has always heard my prayers, and I can trust Him to keep me right where I need to be.

TIME MOVES ON

For the weeks and months following Phil's death, I was in a state of shock. I remember very little. I do remember that only just one week after Phil died, the boys were scheduled to go on a church youth trip.

"Mom, we are going on the youth trip, and we aren't leaving you home," they said. "You're going with us!"

Three busloads of incredible teenagers and chaperones set out for Waco, Texas. For the entire week, we were hugged and loved on. We also went to work, volunteering in the community. This was my first of four youth trips and the beginning of falling in love with both serving and connecting to our church teens.

Over the following years, I found myself especially drawn to the girls. Because of my past, I was able to listen to them without judgment. Because of my current relationship with Jesus and the clean heart He had given me, I had the tools to encourage and build them up, telling them how special they were in God's eyes. I was put in charge of mentoring a group of teen girls, and I am still in contact with several of them to this day. I love them all dearly.

Our home truly became a haven and was always full of Matt and Mark's friends. This brought me so much comfort – until they all went home.

Nights were incredibly hard. More often than not, I sobbed myself to sleep.

Within a brief time of Phil's passing, four other women in our church also lost their husbands. We all had teenage children. Another widow in our church took us under her wing and led us in our grief. I remember her saying, "You didn't just lose a spouse." We'd also lost everything else our spouses were to us – our gardener, mechanic, fix-it person, chef, etc. Most people wear many hats, including our spouses. And when we lost them, we lost all of those things as well. It's hard to quantify the deep void left in the wake of such a loss.

The void was everywhere for me. The boys and their friends filled it for brief periods, but then nighttime came again, and I was all alone.

7/19/03

As this, my third journal comes to a close, I can look back on page one (from 4/21/99) and see that Phil and I were so overjoyed knowing the boys would be in Heaven with us. All Phil ever said to them was, "Just be there." That was the only thing that truly mattered to him.

We always joked and said, "Whoever gets to Heaven first – get it ready for the rest of us!" Well sweetheart, is it beyond description? I know you can't wait to show us the indescribable beauty. After 13 months, do you think it will take forever to comprehend the depth and breadth of God's majesty, or is it instantly understandable?

In 2005, the boys finished high school. In honor of Phil, PCMA provided each of them with scholarships to their universities. They both chose to attend colleges within a day's driving distance of me, but moving them into their respective dorms and leaving them behind was as excruciating as it was exciting, for all of us.

Once the boys were off at college, my focus for serving shifted to behind-the-scenes work; I was part of a chainsaw group that cleared roads after Hurricane Katrina, I volunteered for every church event I could (especially in the huge church kitchen), and I drove the church bus full of students to minister at The Lovelady Center, a home for women just shy of going to prison.

I remember a particularly special night at the Lovelady Center. I had been mentoring a group in a Bible study. I asked the women what they were thankful for and how The Lovelady Center had helped them.

One girl shared how she had become a Christian and realized how special she was in God's eyes. This transformation led her to no longer feeling like she needed to sell herself on the streets to get attention. She was now a child of the King! She then shared that while she was working in the flower shop downtown, a man had come in. He seemed interested in her. Finally, he asked her out on a lunch date.

She shared with our group that this was the first time she had ever gone out with a man where he didn't pay for her body. She was thirty-four years old.

I cried that night, praising Jesus for his mercy on this girl and for her changed life...for *my* changed life!

All I wanted to do was serve wherever I could. I was asked to be on the Jimmy Hale Foundation Board, a homeless ministry in Birmingham. This launched into my time serving the homeless and abused women who lived at Jesse's Place, the female counterpart of the Jimmy Hale Ministry.

Whether I wanted it to or not, time was moving on. In the midst of the indescribable void left by Phil's death, I still had breath in my lungs and a calling on my life. I could choose to use my time for Jesus, or not. Serving is one of God's greatest gifts to us; it gets us outside of ourselves.

I am so thankful that God gave me a heart to serve. I cannot imagine being anywhere or doing anything else.

THE CHRISTIAN LIFE

I've now been a Christian longer than I was not. I've walked with Jesus for thirty-eight years. I've seen God do miraculous things, many of which I've written about in this book. I've seen God answer countless prayers, both in ways I wanted and in ways I'd never want in a million years. Thankfully, I've learned that my circumstances do not determine my relationship with Jesus, nor do they determine whether or not he is good.

God gave me the desire of my heart in my marriage to Phil. So why did God take him away?

I've never gotten an answer to this question. However, as time has gone on, I've realized that I don't need the answer. God knows why He called Phil home, and that's enough for me. I've become content knowing that God's ways are greater than mine and that He does have a plan. Please don't think I was completely fine with God taking him; in no way is that true. I would give almost anything to still have Phil here with us. But God does not guarantee our next breath, and I have become satisfied with that.

Throughout the beginning of this book, I said many times that flying with PSA was the only stability in my life prior to Phil. At the time, this was true. Fortunately, God had other plans for me, and now *He* is the source of my stability and strength.

Some may think that living the Christian life is easy and that actively following Jesus is a no-brainer, even when circumstances are hard. However, this is often not the case.

Eight years after Phil passed away, I was extremely lonely. Our last dog and cat had also died. The boys had graduated college, and Mark had gotten married to his beautiful Rachael. Matt had not yet met Bethany, but he had a wonderful life full of friends and a great job.

In all the years that Phil had been gone, I had not dated a soul. I had been completely focused on the boys, my church involvement, and my job. Finally, I decided to go on a Christian dating site. Many people meet their soulmate this way. I met and talked to many nice people, but one in particular stood out. Out of consideration for him, I will be brief.

Much to the dismay and discouragement of all my friends and family, I got married and divorced over an extremely short period of time. It was an incredibly sad and difficult time. I was the one who ended the marriage – a marriage whose vows were very much centered on Christ. Because I was the one who walked away, my guilt was overwhelming. It manifested itself by me not being able to pray or talk to God for almost a year. Out of shame, I felt I could not face Him .

Finally, in July of 2013, God stepped in and relieved my pain. One day, I heard a prominent Birmingham pastor speaking on the radio. I know God had me listening at that particular time so I could hear from Him .

"Christ did it all. There is nothing you've done that can make Him love you any more, and there is nothing you can do that would make Him love you any less. His love is unconditional."

When I heard the pastor say this, the wall of guilt crashed down and the floodgates of emotions opened up. I realized the blood of Jesus covered all my sins – not just my past, not just this divorce, but all – until I am able to step into eternity and lay at his feet in awe and wonder. I was in tears, and relief and joy swept over me. The next day, God led me to Psalm 51 in my Bible.

In Psalm 51, King David is crying out for forgiveness. He has committed a horrendous sin; he took another man's wife and then killed her husband. David's sin was too much to bear. He fully recognized his sin and cast it before God. Psalm 51 is a prayer of repentance. David is convicted and confesses his sins. Of course, there are consequences; there always are. But there is also cleansing, change, res-toration, gladness, and telling others of God's great mercy. I was experiencing all of this. I wept knowing that I had been forgiven and washed clean once more to praise his holy name.

Repentance opens the floodgates of God's blessings; obedience keeps them open.

Over the course of my life, I have experienced trials and heartaches that have both been my own fault and also been well beyond my control. But through it all, I have discovered the truth of Romans 8:38-39: "For I am convinced that neither death, nor life, nor angels, nor principalities, nor things present, nor things to come, nor powers, nor height, nor depth, nor any other created thing, will be able to separate us from the love of God, which is in Christ Jesus our Lord."

Mark and Rachael moved to Denver in 2011, and I joined them in 2016. Matt and his beautiful wife Bethany recently moved to Salt Lake City. For the first time in ten years, we are all in the same time zone! Upon moving to Denver, I quickly became connected with our church, Mosaic, where I serve on the Connec-tions Team and in the Women's Ministry, leading Bible studies and volunteering. I always tell our pastor's wife that I love being on the Connections Team so that I can know everything that is going on! I'm a constantly curious Enneagram type 7, so this role is perfect for me. I've also gotten involved with the Denver Rescue

Mission and their urban immersion where I've been able to serve the homeless. I've been able to serve sex-trafficked women through Open Door Ministries. We still have strong ties to Birmingham and visit often. We all visit Phil's sisters in California as much as we can.

My heart is full of joy, and I will have a very special volunteer opportunity coming in early 2022 – being a grandmother for the first time to a grandson named Phillip.

Perhaps I'll be called Grandma Goose.

To get the full experience visit

https://www.tijuanatothecross.com/book/photo-experience/

and check out photos and new content now!

TO YOU, MY READERS

Dear Reader, will you meet us in heaven? You may not have tomorrow or your next breath to decide. If God's word is wrong as millions claim, so be it. You've got nothing to lose. When you die, you'll just die. But, if it *is* true as millions of others claim – and countless have lost their lives over – is it worth the risk of not claiming Jesus as your Lord and Savior? What's holding you back? Is it your pride? Your friends? Maybe you feel that you're too smart or educated to believe in this stuff, or that you don't want to be like "those Christians."

I believe with all my soul, to the point of death, that Jesus Christ is the only Savior of the world. This is truly the Word of God that He breathed into me. I pray his word and his breath gives you this same eternal life, peace, and joy! Just ask Him into your life. Your sins will be forgiven. You may be thinking that you don't have any sins. But I can assure you that God is perfect, and you are not. Having Jesus take on all your imperfections is the only way you can stand before the God who created you. My hope is that you will pray the following prayer right now:

Dear God, I am a sinner. There is no way I can stand before the Almighty God without my sins being cleansed. There is no way I can leap across this bottomless chasm that lies between life here on Earth and you, my Holy Redeemer. Yet, in your love and mercy you provide a bridge, a way for me to join you in heaven for all eternity. You gave your one and only son Jesus as the bridge, the sacrifice for my sins, which allows me to cross over into your eternal presence. Father, thank you for sending Jesus Christ to die for me. Forgive me, wash me, cleanse me, and lead me all the days of my life.

If you sincerely prayed this prayer, then you have a huge new family, my friend! We are brothers and sisters in Christ! Read God's word. Start with the book of John. Get connected and involved in your local Christ-centered church. Don't be a burning ember that rolls away and quickly grows dim and cold.

Jesus will give you the meaning of life here on earth, and He will give you hope everlasting, beyond the day you die! He can use your past for his glory! In John 21:25, John tells us that all the books in the world could not contain all that Jesus said and did. However, here are some encouraging things about Jesus that may help you along:

"Truly, truly, I say to you, unless one is born of water and the Spirit He cannot enter into the kingdom of God...you must be born again...so that whoever believes will in Him have eternal life" (John 3:5, 7, 15).

"Truly, truly, I say to you, he who hears My word, and believes Him who sent Me, has eternal life, and does not come into judgment, but has passed out of death into life" (John 5:24).

"I am the bread of life; he who comes to Me will not hunger, and he who believes in Me will never thirst" (John 6:35).

"For this is the will of My Father, that everyone who beholds the Son and believes in Him will have eternal life, and I Myself will raise him up on the last day" (John 6:40).

"Truly, truly, I say to you, he who believes has eternal life" (John 6:47).

"Jesus said, 'I do not condemn you, either. Go. From now on sin no more'" (John 8:11).

"I am the Light of the world; he who follows Me will not walk in the darkness, but will have the Light of life" (John 8:12).

"I am the door; if anyone enters through Me, he will be saved" (John 10:9).

"I am the good shepherd; the good shepherd lays down His life for the sheep" (John 10:11).

"I am the resurrection and the life; he who believes in Me will live even if he dies" (John 11:25).

"A new commandment I give to you, that you love one another, even as I have loved you, that you also love one another" (John 13:34).

"Where I go, you cannot follow Me now; but you will follow later" (John 13:36).

"In my Father's house are many dwelling places; if it were not so, I would have told you; for I go to prepare a place for you. If I go and prepare a place for you, I will come again and receive you to Myself, that where I am, there you may be also" (John 14:2-3).

"I am the way, and the truth, and the life; no one comes to the Father but through Me" (John 14:6).

"For God so loved the world that he gave his one and only Son, that whoever believes in Him shall not perish but have eternal life." (John 3:16).

"Just as the Father has loved me, I have also loved you; abide in my love" (John 15:9).

In Phil's words, "Just be there." Claim Christ's forgiveness, mercy, and grace. See you soon!

TO PHIL

Sweetheart, thirty-five years ago you wanted me to write the evolution of the business traveler. You always thought it fascinating that I began in one era and, like a headwind, blew straight into another. At first, I thought it would just be a fun book, a long reflection of the concept of "Coffee, Tea, or Me." But as our faith in Jesus Christ increased and became a part of everything we did, I realized that there was a bigger parallel happening. I had to talk about the evolution of the business traveler along with my evolution as a Christian.

I went from a hot pants and go-go boots "stew" to a daughter of the King flying first class. You constantly said I could and should write my story – plus, it would make you rich because you would have a famous wife! You always had faith in me. No one ever believed in me, loved me, or encouraged me as much as you did. I just never thought it would take this long to complete. Two things you always said to our boys: "Now go have some fun" (meaning do your best and have a blast doing it), and "Just be there, no matter what. Make the decision of your life to trust Jesus. And when you take that first step into heaven, I'll be there to greet you."

I miss you so my love.
I miss your easy manner. You were so easy to live with, never complaining.
I miss our goodnight hug.
I miss our walks together.
I miss sitting on a restaurant barstool and talking for hours.
I miss you holding my hand.
I miss your cute mischievous smile that says, "I'm adorable. How could you possibly get mad at this face?"
I miss getting excited when you'd come in the door, even after twenty-one years.

I miss the boys and myself running out to your car yelling, "Daddy's home! Daddy's home!" and fighting to see who would get to you first. Then we'd do the sandwich hug with the boys squished in between.

Without a doubt, the boys and I knew how much you treasured your family.

I know that I was your favorite person to spend time with, other than your boys.

Becoming a daddy was the best gift God could have given you. You loved those boys with a joy that no other treasure on Earth could have given you. And you were my gift, my love. Twenty-one years of trials, near bankruptcy (twice), Baba, illness, seven houses, business start-ups, airplanes, and hotels. As we left our sinful pasts, I thank the Lord God that He never gave up on us and that in December of 1984, we knew we had finally come home – our eternal home.

TO SHADES

A special thanks to Shades Mountain Baptist Church and all of the Vestavia Hills families and dear friends who were there for us during Phil's illness and death. Our two youth pastors, Jay Watson and Scott Heath, proved to be an invaluable encouragement to us, unconditionally loving and guiding our boys. Without this loving support, financial aid, and food for months on end, I truly do not know where we would be or what the boys and I would have done. God gave all of you to us for such a time in our lives, and we are forever grateful.

I'M AVAILABLE

I have always felt that I would end up speaking in front of groups, teens, halfway shelters, and women's conferences with some of my uniforms in tow. Men, I'll come speak to you, too! You are so vitally important in how your daughters grow up. I am available for speaking engagements.

To speak with Sandee, please visit https://www.tijuanatothecross.com/contact-us/ and we will reach out to schedule an appointment.

YOUR PAST DOES NOT DICTATE YOUR FUTURE.